Soldier Princess

SOLDIER PRINCESS

*The Life
& Legend of
Agnes Salm-Salm
in North America,
1861–1867*

DAVID COFFEY

TEXAS A&M UNIVERSITY PRESS • COLLEGE STATION

The paper used in this book meets the minimum requirements
of the American National Standard for Permanence
of Paper for Printed Library Materials, z39.48-1984.
Binding materials have been chosen for durability.

Frontispiece: Princess Agnes and Prince Felix Salm-Salm,
c. 1864. *Photo courtesy* Roger D. Hunt Collection,
United States Army Military History Institute, Carlisle Barracks, Pennsylvania.

Library of Congress Cataloging-in-Publication Data

Coffey, David, 1960–
    Soldier princess : the life and legend of Agnes Salm-Salm in North
America, 1861–1867 / David Coffey.— 1st ed.
        p. cm.
    Includes bibliographical references (p.   ) and index.
    ISBN 1–58544–168–6
        1. Salm-Salm, Agnes Elisabeth Winona Leclerq Joy, Prinzessin zu,
    1840– 1912—Homes and haunts—North America.   2. Women—North
America—Biography.   3. Princesses—North America Biography.
4. United States—History—Civil War, 1861–1865—Women.   5. United
States—Social life and customs—19th century.   6. United States—Foreign
relations—Mexico.   7. Mexico—Foreign relations—United States.
8. Mexico—History—European intervention, 1861–1867—Women.
I. Title.
D400.S2C64   2002
970.04'092—dc21   2001005498

For my siblings,

Claire Coffey,

Kevin Coffey,

&

Elizabeth Coffey Farmer

And always,

for my parents

CONTENTS

PREFACE

Remarkable is the adjective most frequently associated with Princess Agnes Salm-Salm, and fittingly so. For even if many of the exploits and honors attributed to her never came to pass, or did so in a less spectacular fashion than she recalled, she lived a remarkable life. Of most of her sixty-eight years (seventy-two by some accounts, sixty-six by others) little is known. But during a ten-year period—from 1862 to 1872—she made her mark. In that time she played an often conspicuous and always colorful role in three of the nineteenth century's major events: the Civil War in the United States, the fall of Maximilian's empire in Mexico, and the Franco-Prussian War. But it remains difficult to determine just how remarkable she might have been.

She appeared seemingly out of nowhere at Washington, D.C., in 1861, an American girl without a past, and she preferred to keep it that way. The prevailing historical impression, reported in numerous reference works and obituaries, holds that she had for some years performed in the circus as an equestrienne. In wartime Washington she married a German soldier of fortune who served in the Union Army and who also happened to be a minor prince. This alone made a good story. But myth took over. By the time of her death in 1912 so many versions of her life, her adventures, even her appearance had emerged that to develop anything like an accurate picture would require magic.

The mythical Agnes became a new-world Florence Nightingale, treating the wounded and campaigning with her warrior husband. She claimed to have been awarded a captain's commission for her Civil War service. Later variations on this theme placed her in command of a company of troops during General William T. Sherman's March to the Sea—the "Soldier Princess." She also claimed a close friendship with President Abraham Lincoln and his family. In an 1899 interview with the *Iowa State Register* she stated that she "knew President Lincoln well, and Mrs. Lincoln. And their little Bob, I have trundled him on my knee many a time."

Available sources, though, tell a different story. While she apparently did care for the sick and wounded in an administrative sense, she likely never nursed anyone during the Civil War and never came under Rebel fire. Nor was she a friend of the first family, although she was known to both the president and the first lady. As for "little Bob," Robert Lincoln—the president's first son—was roughly the same age as Agnes, which puts an entirely different spin on her comment. Even if she accidentally identified the wrong Lincoln child, her statement was ludicrous. Willie Lincoln died in February, 1862, before Agnes could have gained access, and Tad would have been almost ten—a bit past the trundling-on-the-knee stage. Agnes was hardly of advanced age in 1899—fifty-nine at the oldest—and nowhere is there a hint of dementia. It appears that she, too, had bought into the myth.[1]

The troubling thing, from a historical point of view, is that the parts of her life that can be substantiated make for a truly compelling story—how she manipulated powerful men into backing her husband, for instance. In fact, she operated at a high level in what must be considered a man's world. Through her efforts and contacts, she acquired a regimental command for her husband, when his chances for such appeared limited at best. She did use her influence to improve the lives of the sick and wounded—even if she did not toil personally in Civil War field hospitals. She had the ability to attract to her cause several influential friends, among them senators, governors, and generals. In this endeavor she employed her beauty and her charm and, of course, her title.

The impact of her title cannot be dismissed. Lest we believe that America's infatuation with Diana, Princess of Wales, presented a new phenomenon, or, more to the point, that we accept Princess Grace of Monaco as a first among American women, we should consider Princess Salm-Salm. Americans are, after all, supposed to disdain royalty. But this never really has been the case. Indeed, a good many Americans are and always have been enamored of royalty, and this was true during that most republican of times—the Civil War. It is not surprising, then, that much of the exaggeration and myth associated with Agnes Salm-Salm springs from her U.S. career.

Her exploits in Mexico included extravagant and verifiable efforts to save Maximilian from execution, and during the Franco-Prussian War, in which her husband was killed, she took an active and unglamorous role in the relief of the sick and wounded. This is not to suggest that these aspects of her career escaped embellishment. Her attempted sexual seduction of a Mexican officer in a last-ditch plan to facilitate Maximilian's escape remains a popular but unproven vignette from that period. And, although she undoubtedly garnered high recognition for her services to the German army during its war with France, it was widely reported that she received the Iron Cross, one of the most coveted of decorations, which Germany reserved for men only.

Agnes clearly relished the title, but, like Diana and Grace, she often found it hard to stay in character. In a review of her oft-cited book, *Ten Years of My Life*, published in English in 1876, a *New York Times* writer offered an astute observation: "There is evidently no Princess about her, saving only the name, and, doubtless that very fact made her interesting to people unused to so much republican boldness."

There is another undeniable comparison between Agnes and Diana and Grace: sex appeal. By all accounts Agnes was quite physically attractive, perhaps unconventionally so, with something of an Ava Gardner look to her. And like Gardner, she undoubtedly made an impact on men— a lot of men. She caused Abraham Lincoln to blush (and prompted Mrs. Lincoln's overt jealousy in the process); she induced the governor of New York, a man usually immune to female charm, to give her husband the command of a regiment; and she made more than a few soldiers wish they could be in the prince's place. She also warmed the heart of the doomed Maximilian and at the same time stirred the conscience of the victorious Benito Juárez.

Although no evidence has surfaced to prove that Agnes used sex to advance her agenda, there is too much innuendo to ignore. In this regard she resembles another modern woman, the late Pamela Harriman, who gained notoriety for her affairs with great men—a Churchill and a Harriman among them—and for the influence she wielded in political circles. This is not to imply that Agnes had affairs with the great men she encountered, but she certainly made an impression.

So the Agnes who passed into history is largely an invention, one cultivated by the woman herself and perpetuated to the present by chroniclers who proved all too willing to accept the myth. Despite its republican values, America wanted to believe in a warrior princess. The anomaly of a beautiful princess-warrior-nurse made for an irresistible heroine in post–Civil War American culture, just as it would today. The anomalous nature of Agnes Salm-Salm's story likely appealed to a nation that had experienced intense disruptions in traditional gender spheres during the war, as if her achievements exceeded the reach of the average American woman. An exotic princess offered a plausible exception to the rule. In a twist on Voltaire's comment regarding the existence of God: if Agnes had not existed it would have been necessary to invent her, which in a real sense is what happened.

Although tempting, it would be a stretch to cast Agnes as a woman who moved consciously outside of traditional Victorian gender roles. She almost certainly did not think of herself in that way. During a time in which thousands of women aggressively accepted the challenge of nontraditional roles, working as nurses, running family farms, advancing relief efforts, and indeed fighting, Agnes lived the life of a princess. The boldness she exhibited on her husband's behalf, at least during the Civil War, seems to have been little more than youthful impetuosity. Even her activities in Mexico, while clearly less self-serving and undoubtedly courageous, did not represent a substantial challenge to accepted behavior.[2]

But Agnes presents a difficult case in this regard. She clearly behaved unconventionally, and, as will be discussed, she frequently drew the establishment's criticism for such behavior, both in the United States and in Mexico. Then again, once Agnes married a European prince, she instantly threw off myriad potential constraints and created a sphere of her own. After all, how was a teenaged American princess to behave? Her husband apparently harbored no desire for his dynamic bride to conform to a domestic ideal. On one hand, the nature of her public activity, the overt promotion of personal interests, set her apart from women such as Clara Barton, who worked for the general good and in so doing helped to topple the narrow conceptions of the woman's role in society. On the other hand, with her heroic efforts in Mexico, Agnes set a positive example that garnered international praise. Finally, although outside the scope of this work, Agnes earned legitimacy as a wartime caregiver during the Franco-Prussian conflict. Unfortunately, for Agnes and those who would write about her, the more positive aspects of her life paled in comparison to the legend.

Almost ninety years after her death many important details about her life remain unknown. The date and place of her birth cannot accurately be determined. Her life prior to 1861 is the subject of wild speculation because nothing of it is known for sure. This work will not solve these mysteries, although, through a process of elimination, I hope to narrow the range of possibilities.

Something I read in an article about Pamela Harriman in the *Washington Post Magazine* struck me: "After a while, she probably became more myth than woman." What I envisioned as a lively life-and-times story about a "remarkable" woman became more of an attempt to sift through a pile of myth and misinformation in search of some form of truth. There has been a good deal of storytelling about the princess, but almost never is there consensus on any given event or detail. The historical record is hopelessly blurred; apparently no birth record for her exists, and no adequate family history has surfaced. Case in point: one historian—a relative—lists two different birth dates in separate reference works.[3]

But Agnes did write a book, covering roughly a ten-year period from 1861 to 1871, that details her experiences in the Civil War, the Mexican Intervention, and the Franco-Prussian War. It is a colorful, gossipy, self-serving story written by a woman who, after those ten amazing years, was not older than thirty-two and perhaps as young as twenty-six. *Ten Years of My Life* provides the foundation for my study of the first six of those years—the years spent in North America. The rest, her years in Europe, must await a sequel.

Because most writers have accepted her claims and have bought into much of the myth that surrounds her, I have looked to primary documents and newspapers to help sort fact from fiction. I have not altered quotations except to add clarification when necessary and have *not* employed the Latin [*sic*] to identify incorrect or archaic spellings within quotations. Also, I have found it necessary to leave my main subject for several pages at a time in order to establish needed context. While I have failed to confirm some of her claims and have found her in later years to misrepresent her past, the story is not altered substantially by these findings. She remains an interesting, indeed remarkable, woman, who over a ten-year period lived a life that few could imagine and fewer still could match. This book represents at once a search for the real Agnes Salm-Salm and a case study of the impact of invention on history.

ACKNOWLEDGMENTS

The idea to write about Agnes Salm-Salm came to me as I researched a paper on the French Intervention and the Second Mexican Empire for Bill Beezley's Mexican history seminar at Texas Christian University. Dr. Beezley endorsed the idea and encouraged me to pursue it further. The fact that Princess Salm-Salm began her career in the Civil War made her an irresistible subject, allowing me to combine two of my special interests—the Civil War and Mexican history. Her story also prompted me to break from a traditional military study to explore a truly fascinating individual in more of a life-and-times approach, which became my doctoral dissertation and, with a few additions and alterations, this book.

Because a book represents the culmination of a lengthy process that no one can complete without much support and assistance, I am pleased to acknowledge that help. And because there are too few opportunities to do this, I beg the reader's indulgence as I recognize some of the people who have helped me out over the years. Undoubtedly, I have neglected to include the names of many people who deserve mention, and for this I apologize and plead for forgiveness.

During five years of graduate study at TCU I made many friends and accumulated a rather large debt of gratitude. Grady McWhiney, my major professor, allowed me great flexibility in my pursuits and provided me with numerous professional opportunities. I thank him for getting me started in this business of history. Dr. McWhiney's wonderful wife, Sue, died in March, 2000. I remember fondly her sweet spirit and the kindness and encouragement she offered me.

I am fortunate to have worked with some truly excellent professors at TCU. Don Coerver is a gifted scholar and a fabulous classroom teacher. I thank him for his many kindnesses and for setting such a great example. Gene A. Smith, also a great teacher and an aggressive scholar, has been a good friend and supporter. I thank him and his wife, Tracy, for all they've done for me. Steven Woodworth, one of the country's top Civil War historians, has been most helpful. His work has influenced me greatly, and he was kind enough to include a piece I did on the Salm-Salms in his anthology, *The Human Tradition in the Civil War and Reconstruction* for Scholarly Resources. Sara Sohmer, a true asset to the TCU history department, read the manuscript thoroughly and offered some excellent advice.

Thanks to History Department Chair Clayton Brown, former graduate advisor Ken Stevens, and Professor Todd Kerstetter for their kindness and encouragement and to administrative assistants past and present—Barbara Pierce and Dana Summers—who took great care of me over the years. Thanks also to TCU's AddRan College of Arts and Sciences, which supported my graduate education, and to former Associate Deans Priscilla Tate and Bonnie Melhart and Administrative Assistant Ida Hernandez for their assistance.

I am ever grateful to Dr. Beezley, now at the University of Arizona, for his interest and for encouraging me to go to Mexico, where I spent a month improving my Spanish and doing some preliminary research. It was a month that changed my life.

Jim Corder, crafty writer and professor of English at TCU, lost his battle with cancer in 1998. He was a uniquely engaging teacher who served on my master's thesis committee a few years back. I learned a lot from him, and I think about him often. Donald E. Worcester, professor emeritus of history at TCU, remains one of the best writers and editors around. Not only did he teach me so much about writing, but he also gladly read and edited my work, which was a great comfort (and more than a bit humbling). I am honored to know him and thankful for his always gracious assistance.

I wish to thank Spencer Tucker of the Virginia Military Institute (former chair of the TCU History Department) for his support and encouragement and for the opportunity to work on his award-winning *Encyclopedia of the Vietnam War.* It was great experience.

I am privileged to have had some fine colleagues during my time at TCU. Thanks to Mike Nichols, Mark Barringer, Wes Watters, Elizabeth Alexander, Brenda Taylor, Dallas Cothrum, Stan McGowan, Jeff Kinard, and Shannon and Roger Tuller. Special thanks to Mark Beasley for his generous support, and to Matt Esposito and his wife,

Joy, for warm friendship and for Matt's always patient assistance with my many Mexican history questions. Thanks also to Terry Cargill, Eric Osborne, Jay Menzoff, Victor Macias-Gonzalez, Daniel Newcomer, and Claudia Gravier. And thanks to Steve Bunker for his research in Mexican newspapers and for finding me a great place to stay in Oaxaca. James Garza and I were in Mexico together; his help proved invaluable and his friendship is much appreciated. We had a blast.

Tom Mays, now of Quincy University, and his wife, Carrie, have been wonderful friends, with whom I have enjoyed many good times and great adventures. I thank them for being there when it counted. Thanks also to Tom's dad, Bob Mays, who put me up for a night during one of my lonely research trips to Virginia.

A final note about my time at TCU: before I entered the graduate program, Dr. McWhiney invited me to join his Civil War writing seminar. Only days into the semester he suffered a heart attack, but the seminar continued under Don Frazier, with assistance from Marvin Schultz and Bruce Winders. It was a heady experience for me. Schultz and Winders taught me much about writing and seminar etiquette and treated me better than I had a right to be treated. I will never forget their kindness. Thanks especially to Don Frazier, who later invited me to McMurry University in Abilene, Texas, where I taught history for three years and worked on this book. He also read and offered valuable comments on the manuscript.

McMurry University was a great place to work, mostly because of the support I received from Joe Specht and his staff at the Jay-Rollins Library. Warm thanks to Viola Norwood, Trudy Mosley, and especially Lynn Haggard, who worked magic with interlibrary loans. Thanks to Gary Shanafelt of the History Department for helping me with German translations and to Robert Pace of the History Department for his friendship and assistance. Thanks also to Perry Kay Haley for her support and friendship. I am most grateful to all the wonderful people—faculty, staff, and students—who made McMurry such a great place to work.

I formed many friendships in Abilene. Joe and Alice Specht have been terrific. Brandon Polk, a great CPA and burgeoning historian, opened a lot of doors for me. We shared many an adventure. I extend my appreciation to my colleagues at the Abilene Convention Visitors Bureau and on the Texas Forts Trail board of directors. Thanks also to

Bill Whitaker and Loreta Fulton of the *Abilene Reporter-News* and to and my pals at Perini Ranch Steakhouse in Buffalo Gap, Texas.

Lawrence Clayton of Hardin-Simmons University inspired me by example. The popular historian and folklorist died on the last day of 2000, but I will always be thankful for his warm friendship and encouragement.

I am forever indebted to Tarrant County Junior College Professors Cuyler Etheridge, Cindy Baw, and Mike Matthews, who long ago took an active interest in me and encouraged me to continue my education.

And I wish to express my gratitude to my new colleagues at the University of Tennessee at Martin for giving me an exciting new opportunity and a great place to work.

I am grateful to the staffs of many fine libraries and research facilities in the United States and Mexico: the Benito Juárez House, Oaxaca, Mexico; the Library of Congress Manuscript Reading Room, the National Archives, and the Daughters of the American Revolution National Headquarters, all in Washington, D.C.; the New York State Archives and the New York State Library, Albany; the State of Vermont General Services Center, Montpelier; Cody Wright and the folks at the Illinois State Archives, Springfield; the Illinois State Historical Society Library, Springfield; the Rare Book, Manuscript, and Special Collections Library, Duke University, Durham, North Carolina; Ed Skipworth and Ron Becker at Rutgers, State University of New Jersey, Special Collections and University Archives, New Brunswick; the Amon Carter Museum of Western Art, Fort Worth, Texas; The Vineland Public Library, Vineland, New Jersey; the University of Texas Library System, Austin; the Fort Worth Public Library; Mary Couts Burnett Library at Texas Christian University in Fort Worth; Yale University and Beinecke Rare Book and Manuscript Library, New Haven, Connecticut.

Many thanks to the good folks at Texas A&M University Press for having confidence in this unusual story and especially to sales manager Steve Griffis for his friendship and encouragement. I very much appreciate the efforts of copy editor Stephanie Radway Lane and thank everyone who contributed to the production of this book. I am most thankful for the assistance and encouragement of T. Michael Parrish of the Lyndon Baines Johnson Presidential Library in Austin, Texas. And I am grateful for the timely assistance of photo researcher Jim Enos of Carlisle, Pennsylavania.

Many other friends deserve recognition. Thanks to Drake and Mary Bush of Fort Worth. Drake gave me an opportunity to publish my master's thesis and continues to teach me about writing and publishing. Elisa Weidenbaum of Baltimore made my time in Mexico better than I ever imagined it could be and in the process inspired me to push forward with this project. Pam Spraetz of Plano, Texas, long ago gave me an unexpected new lease on life. Jo and Wallace Cox of Haskell, Texas, and their accomplished offspring have been like family for as long as I can remember, for which I am truly thankful.

I have known Robert Heineman for almost twenty-five years. Long ago he taught me the value of hard work, and I have tried to follow the lesson. He is like a brother, and I thank him, his wife, Janis, and their sons, Taylor and Parker, for everything they have done for me.

I am fortunate to have a wonderful family, whose support during the research and writing of this book meant so much to me. Nothing that I write can convey adequately my gratitude. To Lawrence and Sonia Griffith, Neil and Anne Paylor, Kathleen Paylor, Carole (Paylor) and Chip McKibben, Jane and Henry Henegar, Emily (Henegar) Estep, Walter and Anne Henegar, Alexander Henegar, Marilyn and Dick Griffith, Genie and Gary Hendrix, Gwendolin Hendrix, Philip Hendrix, and Elliott Hendrix I offer my love and heartfelt appreciation.

I owe a special debt of gratitude to my cousins, Bob and Johanna Humphrey, who put me up during my research in Washington, D.C., and provided hours of great conversation. And thanks to Johanna's mother, Mrs. Catherine Rose, who for years sent me articles about the Civil War that she cut from newspapers.

I could not have pursued my dream to be a historian in anything like the comfort I have enjoyed without the help of my great aunt, Harrison "Tiny" DeKay. The sister of my maternal grandmother, Aunt Tiny provided financial support that kept me going. She was a fascinating woman, who probably had a lot in common with Agnes Salm-Salm. The wife of a Navy admiral, she got out of Paris before the Nazis moved in, only to find her way to Pearl Harbor. She, like Agnes, lost a loved one—her brother, Colonel Welborn B. Griffith, XX Corps, Third U.S. Army— to enemy fire in France.

This book is dedicated with love to my sister, Claire Coffey, of Woodbridge, Virginia; my brother, Kevin Coffey, who lives with his wife, Tracie, and family in Stromness, Scotland; and my sister,

Elizabeth Farmer, who with her husband, Gary, and their daughters, Julia and Miranda, hold down the family homestead in Fort Worth. My grandparents never got to see my name on a book, but, collectively, they have been a major influence. My greatest inspiration, though, came from my parents, Jerry and Carole Coffey, both gifted writers and editors—people of wonderful tastes and varied interests. And it was only because they supported me unconditionally and on so many levels that I could follow my heart wherever it took me. Like my grandparents, they did not live to see me finish school or publish a book, but I do not write a word or teach a class without thinking about them. I am proud to be their son and pleased to offer this document in their honor.

Soldier Princess

Introduction

This Remarkably Brilliant American Woman

"The Princess Salm-Salm Here," announced the *New York Times* on page one, April 5, 1899. "Woman Who Was Commissioned a Civil War Captain Returns to Visit Old Friends." It had been more than thirty years since she left North America for Europe—and almost that long since she made the American news. Most New Yorkers probably knew little or nothing about this exotically named visitor from Germany. The story provided some background, though, mentioning that she was the widow of Prince Felix Salm-Salm—who fought for the Union during the Civil War, served as chief of staff to Emperor Maximilian in Mexico, and died a hero in the Franco-Prussian War—and that for her efforts on behalf of the Union she received a captain's commission. The reason for her visit, the paper reported, was to return the colors of her husband's former Civil War commands, the 8th and 68th New York Infantry Regiments. She planned an extended stay, with visits to friends and family around the country.[1]

Agnes Salm-Salm still made quite an impression. The *Times* reporter described her as "slender, of medium height," and with hair "more auburn than gray." She had a "bright, pleasant face" and "sparkling eyes." When questioned, she responded freely, betraying perhaps another reason for her visit—the need to tidy up her colorful reputation. She insisted that "it was untrue that she ever thought of going on stage, that it was untrue that she had fallen from a tight-rope in Chicago, and that it was untrue that she had once ridden down Pennsylvania Avenue, Washington, in the uniform of a Captain." So went the popular history of this woman. After a night's rest at the Waldorf-Astoria she proceeded to Vineland, New Jersey, and the home of her younger sister Della and brother-in-law Colonel Edmund Johnson.[2]

If New York welcomed the princess, Vineland rolled out the red carpet. Its *Evening Journal* devoted a good many column inches to her stay, adding confusion to the historical record in the process. Her physical appearance had, it seemed, changed overnight to a "rather stately" five feet, nine inches in height, at a "lithe" 120 pounds. Her "wealth of blonde hair" prompted a curious explanation: "In youth it was black; but several years ago it turned white and since then has been gradually changing to a golden color, a peculiarity of the family." During her visit, the paper reported, Agnes received numerous callers at the Johnson home, and on a brief trip to New York City, she caused quite a commotion at Camden, New Jersey, when "People on the train made a wild rush to get a glimpse of the Princess."[3]

Soon Agnes moved westward to visit old friends. But Vineland followed her progress. "The supposition that Vineland went crazy over Princess Salm Salm's arrival is quickly dispelled," the *Evening Journal* imparted, "when compared with one of the receptions she was accorded during her visit west." The reception mentioned came courtesy of friends and admirers in Des Moines, Iowa, who pulled out all stops. Under the headline "Princess Salm-Salm Coming," the *Iowa State Register* on April 30 included "A Brief Sketch of the Remarkable Career of This Remarkably Brilliant American Woman."[4]

This sketch and a follow-up story a few days later provided the fullest source of information on the mysterious princess since the publication of her book *Ten Years of My Life* in 1876, much of it contradictory. The lead story carried the unfortunately accurate observation that "A history of her life reads like fiction." This sketch offered enough erroneous information to obscure further an already murky history. "She is the heroine of three wars and her influence has, on occasions, positively shaped world events," the sketch began. It included the story of her captaincy and that of her changing hair color. She was, according to the piece, "a notable figure in the set which gathered about the White House." And in reference to the Maximilian episode, the story identified her husband as an Austrian relative of the emperor's and reported that her "hand was in all the tragic events of that international struggle; she held out life for the deluded Austrian, but he would not take it."[5]

The follow-up story included much of this information and more, pieced around highlights of an interview conducted by a woman reporter in "her highnesses' boudoir." Here the reporter revealed that Agnes "was the only lady who was with Sherman in his famous march to the sea," a likely enough story given the friendship with her Des Moines host S. H. M. Byers, author of the popular song "Sherman's March to the Sea." Iowa readers learned that the princess was "Extremely youthful in appearance, bright, vivacious, interesting in conversation," and an avid cyclist. "I love to wheel," Agnes admitted, "I have five wheels, and I am buying a tandem in Chicago. I used to ride one of those high wheels, with a little wheel behind. Funny, weren't they."[6]

Des Moines indeed embraced Agnes Salm-Salm. On May 4, she went for an early spin on her wheel before touring the Iowa Capitol with noted poet Joaquin Miller. The next day Byers and his wife hosted a gala reception—reportedly one of the largest ever given in Des Moines—in honor of the princess, a woman, judging by the lavish coverage of her visit and the inaccurate nature of the stories, no one in Iowa knew very well or bothered to research much at all. Perhaps, they simply took her at face value.[7]

Back East by the end of May, she dropped by New York, where she returned the regimental flags to the survivors of her husband's regiments. She also applied for membership to the New York City chapter of the Daughters of the American Revolution as a descendent of Sergeant Micah Joy of Bridgewater, Massachusetts. Then it was back to Vineland for another reception, "one of the most elaborate affairs of the season." Before returning to Germany in early June, Agnes received yet another honor when the Ladies of the Grand Army of the Republic initiated her into their ranks.[8]

It had been a triumphant visit by any standard. Once again she cap-
tivated America. And once again she spawned wild tales. A French-
language newspaper in Mexico City, *Le Courrier du Mexique,* carried a
bizarre story about how Agnes, while riding her bicycle in New York,
sustained serious head wounds when struck by a tram. Although apparently inaccurate, the story nonetheless testified to Princess Salm-
Salm's ability to stir the imagination.[9]

And then she was gone and once more forgotten. Returned to her
idyllic retirement on the banks of the Rhine, she lived out her years
quietly and entertained American friends, including the famous Clara
Barton, with whom she enjoyed a warm relationship. She returned in
1900 on a mission to raise money for the care of Boer War wounded,
but that trip passed without nearly as much notice. Perhaps her 1899
visit quenched whatever thirst she retained for adulation, or maybe it
allowed her to clear up some unfinished business. But she wanted more
of this visit, more than the return of old flags and a good visit with
friends. It appeared that from the time she landed she intended to re-
mind her homeland about its Soldier Princess, and at the same time
refute some of the unsavory rumors about her past. Possibly, America's
war with Spain the previous year stirred nostalgic feelings. Perhaps she
yearned for the attention that came so freely those many years before.
Whatever her motivation, she clearly relished the return. Moreover,
she left America having so confused the historical record that to fix
anything like a single accurate record of her life would remain beyond
the powers of either newspaper reporters or historians. And that was
just how she wanted it.[10]

In one way or another Agnes bore responsibility for the more mythical Princess Salm-Salm. An unwillingness to discuss her past led to
fantastic speculations about her early life that went too long unanswered,
while her own incredible claims (in her book and later newspaper inter-
views) assured that legend would accompany her name through history.
Of her reticence she wrote, "I must confess it affords me even a mali-
cious pleasure to disappoint, in this respect, a number of persons who
for years have taken the trouble of inventing the most romantic and
wonderful stories in reference to my youth." This represented a selfish
attitude for a public figure—a role she clearly enjoyed—and it left the
curious little alternative but to create a past. Her reticence, later critics

suggested, shielded a disreputable past, when it just as easily could have masked a banal or unpleasant youth. Whatever her reasoning, she opened the door to a plethora of fabrication.[11]

Agnes appeared content to begin her story in 1861, when she first came to Washington in search of adventure. "I am not writing my biography," she told her readers, "I am therefore dispensed from the necessity of describing my cradle, the emotions I experienced in admiring my first pair of shoes, and of dissecting my soul for the amusement of some curious people." The only reference to the past in the pages of her memoir was a cryptic mention of her return from Cuba, where, she wrote, she "had lived for several years." This left the basic details of her life open to speculation—and plenty of it.[12]

By most accounts Agnes Elisabeth Winona Leclercq Joy was born at Swanton, Franklin County, Vermont, or possibly at nearby Philipsburg, Quebec, the fifth child of New England farmer William Joy and his second wife Julia Willard (this marriage produced eight children; William Joy fathered five children with his first wife). According to a history of the Joy family, written by J. R. Joy and published in 1900, Agnes was born on December 25, 1844. But, without noting a discrepancy, J. R. Joy changed the year of birth to 1840 in his sketch of Agnes for the 1935 edition of the *Dictionary of American Biography*. Birth records were kept inconsistently in the 1840s, especially in rural areas, and the Joys apparently did not register her birth. In her book, Agnes stipulated to the Christmas birthday, which she shared with her husband, but she did not mention a year. Yet, in 1899 Agnes told a reporter that she had been only sixteen when she married Prince Salm-Salm in August, 1862, which placed her year of birth in 1845. And there were others: the *Iowa State Register* listed 1846, and the 1888 *Appletons' Cyclopedia of American Biography* gave 1842 as her year of birth.[13]

Stories of Agnes's birth and her formative years abounded. They raged from strange to outlandish and reflected the romantic imagery that she seemed to inspire. A Civil War officer related one version:

> This lady was the daughter of a former English Colonel, who, being a passionate hunter, had left the service and joined the Hudson Bay Fur Company. For years he lived in the far West of Canada as a nimrod, and there married a very pretty Indian squaw, daughter of a

chief, and known as "The Princess." When quite young his daughter was stolen by some Indian enemy and sold to a circus manager, who had noticed her riding a wild broncho on the plains. He took her away with him to Cuba and South America, and after a time she became a most daring rider of bareback horses, and attracted much attention on the account of her brilliant eyes and lovely form. Still, this is only one version of her life, and it may not be true at all.

Another version, by the formidable *Appletons' Cyclopedia*, offered a vastly different account, beginning with her place of birth, listed as Baltimore. And in a testimony to her obscurity after the 1870s, the respected reference work reported her death "in Coblentz, Germany, about 1881." The entry continued, informing readers that Agnes was "said to have been adopted when a child in Europe by the wife of a member of the cabinet at Washington, but after receiving a good education in Philadelphia, to have left her home and become a circus-rider and then a rope-dancer. Afterward she acquired a reputation as an actress under the name of Agnes Leclercq, and lived several years in Havana, Cuba." This all before she returned to the United States in 1861, when, according to the *Cyclopedia*, she would have been nineteen. Even her *New York Times* obituary included a hodgepodge of misinformation: that she was the daughter of an "American Colonel named Leclercq," that she was born in Baltimore in 1840, and that she had been an actress.[14]

Agnes may have fostered these divergent renditions of her life; and she certainly contributed to the embellishment of her wartime exploits, but clearly her 1899 visit included a quest to set the record straight, at least as far as it concerned her American family. "There was that dreadful story about my being a circus rider," she told an Iowa reporter. "Not that it has annoyed me a particle. I never cared. If it had been true I would have said 'Why, yes I was once in a circus,' but it isn't." It annoyed her relations, though, she admitted, "and it is for them that I wish it righted."[15]

True or not, the circus rider story persisted. She explained that it came from a *New York Herald* reporter in Mexico, who on witnessing her daring horsemanship suggested that she must have been raised in a circus. Her riding ability attracted much admiration and indeed fueled reports of a circus performer past. As President Lincoln's friend Noah Brooks noted, "It was said that her well-known skill and deftness in the care and management of horses were acquired when she was a circus-rider; at that period of her checkered career she was billed as 'Miss Leclerq.'"[16]

As a name, Agnes Elisabeth Winona Leclercq Joy was bound to stand out, especially when followed by Princess Salm-Salm. And, as a name, it sent chroniclers in all sorts of directions. Again, Agnes helped to confuse the case. When she arrived at Washington, and when she married Prince Salm-Salm, she went by the name of Agnes Leclercq, which could have represented an attempt to protect her family from embarrassment in the event of her disreputable behavior or a desire to separate herself from that family, or maybe she just liked the sound of it; it certainly sounded more exotic than Joy. Whatever her motivation, it led to the assumption that she descended from French or French-Canadian stock, or as the *New York Times* reported, from an "American Colonel named Leclercq."[17]

With regard to her personal and family histories, as with other aspects of her life, the story needed no embellishment. Agnes descended from solid Yankee stock. The Joy family's American progenitor, Thomas Joy, came to Boston in 1635; Agnes's great grandfather Nathaniel Joy was killed in the French and Indian War, and her grandfather Micah Joy fought during the American Revolution. Her father farmed in the Lake Champlain region of Vermont and Quebec for dozens of years. During her 1899 visit, Agnes could count Joy siblings and cousins among the respected citizens of St. Louis, Detroit, Chicago, and New York. Yet for most of her adult life, she appeared to shun that family. Except for her sister Della, with whom she appeared quite close, Agnes made no mention of family in her book and apparently had little contact with them in the years before her return. The 1899 visit, then, represented a true homecoming—an attempt to reclaim a family she had once, for whatever reason, abandoned.[18]

For those who encountered Agnes during the Civil War and in Mexico, or those who sought to write about her later, this sort of respectable, truly American pedigree just would not do. She was too unconventional, too spirited, and, by some accounts, too unprincipled, not to have an exotic story, be it circus rider or Indian princess. Agnes must have been content with such speculation, as she did nothing to discourage it. And if she disliked the specific references, she certainly enjoyed the mystery they fostered—at least until 1899, when she tried to put the circus story to rest for the benefit of her family—and by then nobody was listening. "Forty-four years ago [1855] I was a little girl in short skirts, living with my sister, Mrs. [Edward] Mendel, in Chicago," she told an Iowa reporter. "When I was [fifteen] years old I went to Washington to visit another sister," she continued, "and there I met my husband. I met him in '61 and married him in '62. I was just sixteen years old then."[19]

This was vintage Agnes. The statement may have satisfied her family's concerns, but it did nothing to clear up her historical record. Even as she sought to refute one inaccuracy she created others, namely her age. She also left a six-year gap—plenty of time for a turn in the circus or a flirtation with acting; and she made no mention of Cuba, where she had, according to her book, spent "several years" before returning to the United States in 1861. Whether or not Agnes rode horses in a circus in Cuba or acted on stage in New York made no difference, because when she arrived in Washington during the Civil War's first year she stood poised for a complete makeover. Nothing in her past could compete with what lay ahead. For all intents and purposes Agnes Salm-Salm had yet to be born.

CHAPTER 1

The Sweet Malady

"The great American civil war had commenced, the first battle of Bull Run had taken place, and the whole American world was in an incredible fever of excitement," wrote Agnes Salm-Salm of the time that changed her life. As the center of activity for the Union, Washington attracted sightseers, opportunists, would-be soldiers, and women from all over the country; Agnes "was as eager and enthusiastic as the rest" to share the experience. She arrived at the capital in the fall of 1861 to witness a grand cavalry review. "Military enthusiasm was paramount in Washington," and ladies "were not left untouched by the prevailing epidemic," she quipped; "Apollo himself would have passed unnoticed if he did not wear shoulder-straps." And young Agnes was as "favorably disposed towards the uniform as other ladies."[1]

Agnes and the other women who came to the nation's capital that fall in search of husbands, adventure, or income could not have picked a more opportune time. The disastrous performance of the Federal army at Bull Run convinced Americans on both sides of the conflict that the war would not be settled quickly or easily. President Abraham Lincoln had called for more volunteers, and soldiers from across the Union flocked to the capital. The primary marshaling point for Federal armies in the East, Washington received regiment after regiment as states released them for government service. Bull Run demonstrated graphically the lack of preparedness that plagued Federal forces, and Lincoln moved decisively to correct the problem. He demoted his Bull Run commander, the unfortunate Brigadier General Irvin McDowell, and placed the entire army and the hopes of the Union in the hands of thirty-five-year-old Major General George B. McClellan. The impressive but little-tested McClellan worked diligently to build the Army of the Potomac, which now bore little resemblance to the battered force that scrambled away from Manassas Junction in July, 1861.

The swelling Army of the Potomac occupied camps in and around Washington and across the river in Northern Virginia. "To visit around Washington was then the fashion," Agnes recalled. After witnessing the cavalry review, which left her "quite bewildered by the perfectly new spectacle" (in retrospect she rated the Union cavalry "worse than useless" compared to the Prussian hussars of her later experience), Agnes with a party of fellow spectators crossed the Potomac into Virginia to visit some of the camps. One cantonment, that of flamboyant Brigadier General Louis Blenker's "German Division," became a favored destination for civilian visitors and Army brass alike. "The camp of the German division," Agnes allowed, "was at that period the principal point of attraction."[2]

Admired for its martial appearance and grand hospitality, Blenker's camp featured fine food and drink, as well as a sizable complement of exotic officers. "German," a label liberally applied to almost any soldier of non-English-speaking origin, in this case described a truly ethnic division composed of Germans, Poles, Hungarians, and others of European origins. General McClellan exaggerated only slightly when he wrote that the division included "Zouaves from Algiers, men from the 'Foreign Legion,' Zephyrs, Cossacks, Garibaldians of the deepest dye, English deserters, Sepoys, Turcos, Croats, Swiss, beer drinkers from Bavaria, stout men from North Germany, and no doubt Chinese, Esquimaux, and detachments from the army of the Grand Duchess of Gerolstein." Blenker, himself a refugee from the German revolutions of 1848, maintained an extended staff that included fellow refugees, soldiers of fortune, and several lavishly attired noblemen, "shipwrecked Germans," as Agnes called them.[3]

Blenker's camp made quite an impression on visitors, including one regular, General McClellan:

> The most entertaining of my duties were those which sometimes led me to Blenker's camp. . . . As soon as we were sighted Blenker would have the "officer's call" blown to assemble his polyglot collection, with their uniform as varied and brilliant as the colors of the rainbow. Wrapped in his scarlet-lined cloak, his group of officers ranged around him, he would receive us with the most formal and polished courtesy. Being a very handsome and soldierly-looking man himself, and there being many equally so among his surroundings, the tableau was always very effective, and presented a striking contrast to the matter-of-fact way in which things were managed in the other divisions.
>
> In a few minutes he would shout, *"Ordinanz numero eins!"* whereupon champagne would be brought in great profusion, the bands would play, sometimes songs be sung.

Into this heady environment went Agnes Leclercq Joy. According to her, the camp presented a fine appearance, laid out in "German fashion," with tents arrayed in neat rows and freshly planted trees along the lanes that separated the regiments.[4]

She and her fellow visitors arrived at Blenker's headquarters, where the general offered his now famous hospitality. Agnes developed a high regard for her host and his deportment, believing that he resembled "half a Prussian commanding general, half a Turkish pasha."[5]

At Blenker's tent Agnes noticed a late-arriving staff officer, whom the general presented as "Colonel Prince Salm." She described a man of "middle height," with an "elegant figure, dark hair, light moustache, and a very agreeable handsome face, the kind and modest expression of which was highly prepossessing." He appeared bashful and wore a monocle on his right eye. "I felt particularly attracted by the face of the Prince," Agnes recalled, "and it was evident that my face had the same effect on him." Although the prince spoke no English and she knew nothing of German or French, they managed to communicate in "the more universal language of the eyes, which," she admitted, "both of us understood."[6]

Born at Anholt, Westphalia, in 1828, like Agnes on Christmas Day, Felix Constantin Alexander Johann Nepomuk, Prince Salm-Salm was the younger brother of the reigning Prince zu Salm-Salm. One of six lines in a dynastic family whose origin dated to the tenth century, the Salm-Salm line administered a small principality on the lower Rhine River, near the Dutch border southeast of Arnhem, from its seat at Bocholt. Part of the Holy Roman Empire, the mediatized principality joined Napoleon's Confederation of the Rhine in 1806 before falling under Prussian hegemony in 1815.[7]

Salm received a military education at Berlin, and as a young subaltern in the Prussian cavalry he was seriously wounded while fighting the Danes in Schleswig-Holstein. Perhaps spoiled by his father's generosity and with easy access to his family's wealth, Salm spent carelessly and entertained in grand style. After his father's death, he quickly exhausted his inheritance and accumulated a princely debt. According to one contemporary, the prince "was one of the most high-toned and cavalier-like persons in Europe, but he was wonderfully extravagant." To escape his creditors he joined the Austrian army only to repeat his financial frivolity—a prince simply could not live on a junior officer's pay, not in Vienna. When the new reigning prince refused to pay his spendthrift brother's rising debts, Salm looked across the Atlantic to America, where war beckoned.[8]

Carrying letters of recommendation and backed by Prussian military mystique, Salm arrived at Washington and offered his sword to Federal authorities, who gratefully accepted his services. The contradiction was not lost on Agnes, who later wrote, "Though republicans, the American people were no enemies to princes. . . . A live prince was an object of great interest to both gentlemen and ladies." His inability to speak English, however, created an obstacle. Secretary of War Simon Cameron offered him the command of a Kentucky cavalry regiment, but Salm felt uneasy about his ability to communicate. He hoped for a place in one of the German regiments. He settled for an honorific colonelcy on Blenker's inflated staff, which in light of that group's size, made it a precarious position from the start.[9]

While Blenker welcomed old-country aristocrats, Prussian noblemen, regardless of merit, attracted the contempt of other, more radical "Forty-eighters" in the division. This manifested itself in the form of political backbiting and charges of corruption against Blenker. To make matters worse, the War Department soon cracked down on opulent staffs, leaving Salm's future in the army very much in doubt.[10]

If the Civil War was, as Agnes suggested, a "godsend" to the many "shipwrecked Germans," Agnes was a godsend to Salm. Recalling their first meeting, she wrote, "When I left General Blenker's camp I left behind an enamoured Prince." They saw each other often over the next few weeks and the "sweet malady increased."[11]

But in March, 1862, Salm took the field with Blenker's command when it moved into western Virginia to join Major General John C. Frémont's ill-fated Mountain Department. After a miserable journey, during which it got lost and ran out of supplies, the German Division arrived in time to share the suffering occasioned by Confederate Major General Thomas J. "Stonewall" Jackson's brilliant Shenandoah Valley Campaign. Following a rough showing in the Battle of Cross Keys that June, Blenker's German Division was ordered back to northern Virginia as part of Major General John Pope's newly formed Army of Virginia. But on Blenker's return to the Washington area, controversy, political intrigue, and the failure of the recent campaign, although hardly his fault, combined to topple the fiery German—apparently his penchant for European royalty on his staff angered too many of the old Forty-eighters. Relieved in June, Blenker awaited a new assignment that never came. (Without a command, Blenker resigned his commission in March, 1863, and retired to his farm in New York, where he died only months later.) This left Salm without a job and his future in America uncertain at best.[12]

While Salm toiled in the field, Agnes remained in Washington. She recalled that the two carried on a "most lively correspondence" in English, with which Salm showed progress. During his absence Agnes worked diligently on his behalf. "I soon became aware that we could never progress or succeed much in America," she wrote, "without the help of influential friends." And Agnes proved remarkably adept at acquiring influential friends.[13]

After his return from the Shenandoah in June, Salm also attempted to curry favor in Washington. Along with his friend and fellow German Division staffer Colonel Otto von Corvin, Salm presented to President Lincoln an ambitious plan to bring 20,000 volunteers, presumably trained soldiers, from Germany to fight for the Union. The plan required the U.S. government, essentially, to pay passage for the German recruits, who would be emigrants, pay them soldiers' wages, and provide them with some land upon the expiration of their term of service. To avoid international conflict, Salm and Corvin would operate as independent recruiting agents in Germany. Once several thousand troops had been mustered, Salm would have a command—and not just a regiment, for even if he brought a quarter of the proposed 20,000, he could expect at least a brigade and possibly a division. Lincoln appeared intrigued and endorsed the plan on August 15. Anything that could bolster his army without calling for more American boys held appeal, but reality encroached. Several thousand German mercenaries might recall the hated Hessians of the Revolutionary War, and many Americans objected to the large numbers of foreign troops already in the army, especially Germans and Irishmen, who constituted a substantial bloc. Too, logistical and financial support for such an effort would be daunting. Agnes maintained that in addition to Lincoln's approval, Secretary of State William Seward enthusiastically supported the plan; however, new Secretary of War Edwin Stanton, "who was utterly disgusted with foreigners," refused to go along.[14]

Time, distance, and unemployment failed to dampen the romance, which spoke well for Agnes's character. On August 30, 1862, as his former division fought a second battle at Bull Run, the prince married Agnes in a private Catholic ceremony at Washington's St. Patrick's Church. The irony proved too rich for a fellow Teuton Unionist, who wrote of the marriage, "So the Indian Princess became a German Princess, and the wife of a man whose ancestral tree went way back to the Crusaders." The newlyweds understood that Salm's career in the Union army depended on his ability to land a state-issued commission and regiment to command. Anything less than a colonelcy must have been unthinkable. To this end the royal couple departed for Albany, New York, where Agnes planned to exert some influence of her own.[15]

She had good reason for optimism. In Albany Agnes called on U.S. Senator Ira Harris, one of the influential friends she had cultivated in Washington. The sixty-year-old Harris, a well-connected Republican, proved a valuable ally, securing for the princess an audience with Republican Governor Edwin Morgan. The senator, whom Agnes found "a great friend of the Germans," even agreed to accompany her. Incredibly, Salm did not even attend the meeting, persuaded that his weak grasp of English would endanger the mission.[16]

Nor was his presence required; Agnes managed quite nicely without him. Although Harris warned her that Morgan possessed "the reputation for being a woman-hater," Agnes won over the governor with a passionate appeal. Morgan wielded great power during the war's early years; in addition to his civil authority he held a major general's commission in the U.S. Volunteers as commander of the Department of New York. Under his leadership, New York sent more than 200,000 troops into Union service. In short order Morgan presented Agnes with a colonel's commission for Salm. She had delivered her husband a regiment, a German regiment at that—Blenker's own 8th New York Volunteer Infantry.[17]

In November, 1862, Salm left Albany to join his new command in northern Virginia, and a few days later Agnes followed him; but once in camp, they received a less than cordial welcome. The regiment, at least some of its officers, bitterly opposed Salm's appointment, notice of which preceded the triumphant couple's arrival. In a letter to Governor Morgan dated October 23, 1862, members of the 8th New York voiced their disapproval. The protest did not center on Salm's title, although it doubtless fanned the flames of discontent. As a Prussian officer he represented the enemy to many of the former revolutionaries. It focused rather on his outsider status; he had not fought with them at First Bull Run or, more important, at Second Bull Run, when he presumably enjoyed his wedding night. The authors advanced one of their own, Lieutenant Colonel C. B. Hedterich, who led the regiment at Second Bull Run, as the proper choice. One major, seven captains, eight first lieutenants, eight second lieutenants, the regimental adjutant, and the regimental surgeon signed the protest. Brigade commander Colonel Leopold von Gilsa, division commander (and former commander of the 8th) Brigadier General Julius Stahel, and XI Corps commander Major General Franz Sigel added endorsements.[18]

A pamphlet that contained the protest, organized and published by Captain Gustav Struve, also included the aggrieved Hedterich's complaint and those of prominent New York Germans, who portrayed Salm as unfit for command. It also suggested that Governor Morgan would not have made the appointment had he known of the dissatisfaction with Salm. To make matters worse, once Salm and Agnes arrived in camp, the officers had to endure the new princess's obnoxious behavior. According to the pamphlet, she made no secret of the fact that she, not

Salm, had secured the position and that she could see to other personnel dispositions as well. For the fifty-seven-year-old Struve, a leader of Baden's 1848 revolts against Prussia and an important figure in America's German community, the combination proved more than he would tolerate. The pamphlet he published included his resignation.[19]

Agnes mentioned nothing of this inauspicious beginning to her husband's command when she reflected on the glorious opening phase of her own career. But then she had little time to enjoy camp life. While she and Salm had campaigned in New York that September, McClellan's Army of the Potomac fought the Battle of Antietam—the bloodiest single day in American history—and turned back Confederate General Robert E. Lee's first invasion of the Union. McClellan's failure to exploit the perceived opportunity to destroy Lee's army led to his exit from the war. In November, under extreme pressure, McClellan's successor Major General Ambrose Burnside launched his disastrous Fredericksburg Campaign, which meant active operations for Salm and prompted Agnes's return to Washington. The 8th New York, part of Hungary-born General Stahel's First Division, XI Corps, escaped the wintry carnage at Fredericksburg in December. Shortly thereafter a lull in the fighting allowed Agnes to rejoin her husband in time to celebrate their mutual birthday.[20]

Circumstances dictated a shabby affair by royal standards, or any other standard for that matter, but, according to Agnes, the entire division pitched in. General Stahel sent a band and soldiers prepared a finely decorated mud cake, which she took as joke but could have just as easily been an unpleasant message. Dining fare consisted of salt pork and hardtack. "With the utmost difficulty," she recalled, "Salm procured four bottles of very vile whisky," to which they added sugar and lemons, producing "a most abominable, abundantly watered stuff." The makeshift party, nonetheless, had a decidedly pleasing effect.[21]

"Mrs. Slam Slam"

The royal couple and their guests may well have enjoyed that Christmas of 1862, but they represented a minority in the Army of the Potomac. McClellan's ouster, followed by the slaughter at Fredericksburg, sent an ill wind though the army that "Little Mac" had done so much to build.

Factionalism divided the command, and much of the army's top brass openly opposed Burnside, who in turn lacked confidence in himself. With only the nominal victory at Antietam standing amid two humiliating defeats at Bull Run, a repulse before Richmond during the Seven Days' Battles, and, most vividly and most recently, Fredericksburg, the Union's highest profile fighting force sank to a new low. Yet plans for another push against Lee's position in northern Virginia went forward.[22]

The Salm-Salm birthday festivities became a distant memory once General Burnside again took the offensive in a desperate effort to dislodge the Confederates from their Rappahannock River line. Burnside hoped to move around Lee's flank by crossing the river upstream from Fredericksburg, leaving the Confederate stronghold untenable. Soft rains that began on January 20, 1863, came in freezing sheets by nightfall, turning the region into a quagmire that swallowed mules and sucked down wagons and guns. Soldiers were little better off. The so-called "Mud March" brought a fitting conclusion to the campaigning season, and a merciful end to Burnside's tumultuous tenure as army commander.[23]

Agnes shared the hardships of the Mud March, and remained with the army as it slogged toward a new encampment at Aquia Creek, not far from the Fredericksburg battleground. The Salm-Salms settled into winter quarters at Aquia Creek and there fashioned a temporary home of considerable opulence—even for the now abundantly provisioned Army of the Potomac. Agnes recalled that "Salm procured a large hospital tent, which was decorated very tastefully and even gorgeously; for amongst the soldiers of his regiment were workmen of all trades." These warrior-decorators lined the tent walls with colorful damask; the salon featured carpeting and a "splendid sofa," to which Salm added a large mirror that attracted the "admiration of everybody." The bedroom looked "splendid" as well: "the soldiers had made of boards a large bedstead, and provided it with a straw mattress, over which was spread a buffalo skin, and another, together with blankets, served as a coverlet. Over our heads arched a canopy, decorated with white and red damask, and the whole looked quite grand." A separate kitchen tent housed a "negro servant girl," whom Agnes had brought from Washington. "We had our own caterer, who provided us with all the delicacies of the season," the princess confided, "and our wine cellar, which was dug in the ground, contained bottles of the most different shapes and contents."[24]

In late January Major General Joseph Hooker replaced the unfortunate Burnside, ushering in a period of frivolity seemingly staged to show-
case Agnes, Princess Salm-Salm. Hooker, Burnside's chief critic, brought
with him solid credentials as a fighter and the not-so-welcomed reputation of a heavy drinker and womanizer. Under his command the army's
winter camps assumed an often unmilitarily festive aspect. Liberalized
visitation rules brought officers' families from throughout the Union
and soon the camps were, according to Agnes, "teeming with women
and children." This made for a lively social season. "Scarcely a day passed
without some excursion, pleasure party, dinner, or ball." Hooker also
instituted numerous reforms designed to improve the soldiers' lives and
bolster his army's morale. Almost overnight, at least as far as a good
number of officers and men were concerned, the gloom lifted from the
Army of the Potomac.[25]

As resident celebrities Colonel and Mrs. Salm played a conspicuous
role on the winter party circuit, but the season's master of ceremonies
became ever-controversial III Corps commander Major General Daniel
Sickles. A colorful New York politician, Sickles had been acquitted for
murdering his wife's lover, Philip Barton Key, son of "Star Spangled
Banner" composer Francis Scott Key. As a Democrat who supported
the war effort, he received consideration from Lincoln and managed to
push into the army's high command. His promotion to corps command
was viewed by some as early evidence of his friend Hooker's malfeasance. Still, Sickles could entertain with the best. Agnes described one
event:

> This immense tent was decorated inside and outside with flags,
> garlands, flowers, and Chinese lamps in great profusion, and offered
> a fairy-like aspect. The supper laid under the tent for about two hun-
> dred persons, ladies and gentlemen, could not have been better in
> Paris, for the famous Delmonico from New York had come himself
> to superintend the repast, and brought with him his kitchen aides
> and batteries, and immense quantities of the choicest provisions and
> delicacies, together with plate and silver, and whatever was required
> to make one forget that it was a camp supper. The wines and liquors
> were in correspondence with the rest, and no less, I suppose, the bill
> to be paid.

She opined that the "unheard-of luxury displayed on this occasion" would not have been tolerated in a European camp, but things were "far different in America." Apparently, Agnes lost her grasp on reality once she took on a title; she mistakenly believed that "Soldiers and people liked and approved such displays," and that "soldiers did not grudge the generals their luxurious habits either; they found an amusement in such festivals, and were sensible enough to understand that they could not all partake in them." The reason for the soldiers' sensible acceptance, she maintained, rested in the fact that their government took such good care of them. Then again, the Soldier Princess had yet to see any fighting.[26]

Most of what Agnes knew of military life to this point concerned its more pleasant aspects, and nothing happened at Aquia Creek to change her perception. As winter gave way to spring social opportunities abounded, and the Salm-Salm tent became the sight of frequent receptions. In March officers from Sickles's III Corps organized a day of sporting events and horse races attended by Hooker and other important officers. During one race Salm was thrown from his mount and, according to one observer, "came near breaking his neck." Agnes, on the other hand, managed to dazzle observers with her riding ability. Colonel Charles Wainwright, I Corps chief of artillery, noted the large number of women present: "Mrs. Salm-Salm and Mrs. Farnum [wife of Colonel J. E. Farnum], of course, were on hand. Both have been handsome women in their day, and are still good-looking enough to stand very well in the eyes of General Joe [Hooker]. The camps are full of stories about them both."[27]

Such remarks were likely to follow any woman who, married or not, too closely associated herself with Generals Hooker or Sickles. The puritanical Charles Francis Adams, Jr., grandson of President John Quincy Adams, then a captain in the 1st Massachusetts Cavalry, echoed the opinion of many soldiers and civilians alike when he wrote that "the Headquarters of the Army of the Potomac was a place to which no self-respecting man liked to go, and no decent woman could go. It was a combination of barroom and brothel." Agnes's physical beauty, combined with her bold, assertive personality and an evident preference for male company, made her a prime target for, if nothing else, guilt by association. Of one assembly at Sickles's headquarters, Colonel Robert McAllister of the 11th New Jersey Infantry wrote to his wife, "In my next letter I will tell you something as to how the ladies looked—and also about Mrs. Salm Salm, sometimes called Mrs. Slam Slam. I just learned yesterday who she was." Unfortunately, Colonel McAllister never finished the thought, but the implication if not sexual in nature was almost certainly negative. She undoubtedly sparked a good deal of innuendo.[28]

But the spirited Agnes left a more martial impression on one future hero. Brigadier General Joshua Lawrence Chamberlain of Maine, who gained fame at Gettysburg and amassed a stellar record during the war, evoked fondly that halcyon spring of 1863 in his eerie memoir *A Passing of the Armies*. Writing shortly after the war, after two years of intense fighting and a life-threatening wound, Chamberlain recalled "Princess Salm-Salm the Valkyrie," a reference to the warrior maidens of Norse legend.[29]

Her leading role in the season's crowning event only enhanced whatever reputation she had, and, as usual, her performance produced several reviews and little consensus. In April, before spring campaigning commenced, President and Mrs. Lincoln with son Tad paid a visit to Hooker's army. After reviewing the troops the president attended a reception arranged by General Sickles. In an effort to buoy the president's obviously low spirits, Sickles persuaded a group of officers' wives to shower Mr. Lincoln with affection. According to one account, "The Princess Salm-Salm, a very beautiful woman, led the way. . . . A glance from the princess toward the ladies in her train was all that was necessary." The petite Agnes stood on her tiptoes and, pulling Lincoln's head downward, kissed him on the cheek. "If a squadron of cavalry had surrounded the president and charged right down upon him, he could not have been more helpless." Lincoln's friend Noah Brooks wrote that Agnes "astonished the President, on his entering General Sickles's headquarters, by flying at him, and planting a bouncing kiss on his surprised and not altogether attractive face." Brooks also suggested that "Princess Salm-Salm had laid a wager with one of the officers that she would kiss the President. Her audacious sally won her a box of gloves." Agnes made scant reference to the president's visit and offered no acknowledgment of her starring role, but she devoted several pages of her memoir to Lincoln—a man she clearly admired.[30]

Mrs. Lincoln, who had not been present at the time but learned of the reception episode later in the day, refused to speak to General Sickles when he escorted the first family back to Washington. Over dinner, the story went, Lincoln tried to break the ice, saying, "Sickles, I never knew that you were such a pious man." The general politely assured Lincoln that he was mistaken; to which Lincoln replied: "They tell me you are the greatest Psalmist in the army. They say you are more than a Psalmist—they say you are a Salm-Salmist." At that, Mrs. Lincoln gave in and forgave the general.[31]

Sickles had indeed become a Salm-Salmist—an enthusiastic advocate for Colonel Prince Salm. In a letter to President Lincoln, he evoked the names of famous foreign soldiers in American service—the Marquis de LaFayette and Baron von Steuben of the Revolutionary War—to urge Salm's promotion to brigadier general. On what evidence Sickles based this lofty comparison he did not mention, nor could he offer much in the way of specific examples—Salm had commanded a regiment for only five months and had never led U.S. troops into battle. "This is the first instance in which I have ventured to address a recommendation to the Government in behalf of any officer not serving in my own command," Sickles wrote, before getting to the heart of the matter: "The regiment which Colonel Salm commands will be mustered out of service in the latter part of April. Unless promoted to the rank of brigadier-general, for which he is abundantly qualified, the service will lose in his unwilling retirement one of its most accomplished and faithful officers." Apparently, Agnes had acquired another influential friend.[32]

The threat to Salm's continued employment, though, was all too real. The 8th New York Volunteer Infantry mustered into Federal service for a two-year enlistment on April 23, 1861. Even with the anticipation of renewed fighting on a grand scale, the government honored enlistment expirations, however untimely. So as Agnes entertained the president and stirred imaginations throughout the Army of the Potomac, she knew that time was running out. She likely engineered Sickles's appeal for a promotion and doubtless pursued other men of influence for similar favors. Promotion offered one way—the obviously preferable way—for Salm to stay with the army, because general officers were not subject to enlistment confines and served at the discretion of the Federal government. Another possibility meant a repeat of Agnes's earlier performance—to find a governor who would give Salm another regiment. The only other prospect was for the 8th to reenlist *en masse*, but the regiment's unfavorable reaction to Salm's colonelcy, among other unpleasant memories, made this most unlikely.[33]

With no promotion forthcoming, Salm dutifully prepared to accompany his men back to New York, where the regiment would muster out. Agnes, meanwhile, went to Washington to plead her husband's case—to no avail. The 8th passed through the capital city, where they "were received with much cheering." The men formed in ranks and, according to Agnes, "the whole procession, headed by myself and a numerous cortége, marched across Washington to the New York railroad depôt." Then they moved on to New York, where the citizens welcomed their returning warriors, who, according to Agnes, presented their colonel with a "magnificent sword of honor, with a solid golden scabbard and hilt with silver ornaments." Perhaps those officers had not spoken for the men back in November, or perhaps Salm won them over—by most accounts he was a good, decent, and loyal man. At a party for the former soldiers, Agnes recalled, "I was of course toasted, and when Salm rose to answer, he was silenced by the clamorous demand for a speech from me. I had to comply, and my efforts to express myself in German were received with thundering applause." For her, this "ended a very pleasant, rather too short, period of my American life, and one of trouble and anxiety commenced." She had to be one of few people associated with the Union war effort to find 1862 and early 1863 pleasant.[34]

Her departure from the Army of the Potomac did not go unnoticed. "We are all sorry that Mrs. *Salm-Salm* has left the army," wrote Lieutenant Frank Haskell of Brigadier General John Gibbon's staff, adding sarcastically, "She is a beautiful woman and the presence of *ladies* is so charming in camp, to chasten the morals and manners of the men."[35]

CHAPTER 2

The End Justifies the Means

The discharge of Salm's regiment proved fortuitous for commander and men alike. Only days after they marched out of their Virginia camps, the expected campaign season opened in the woods west of Fredericksburg. The Battle of Chancellorsville that first week of May, 1863, became the latest in a line of humiliating defeats for the Army of the Potomac. In General Lee's "masterpiece," his outnumbered Army of Northern Virginia rocked the Federals with a devastating flank attack delivered by Stonewall Jackson. After securing his position, a dazed Hooker withdrew across the Rappahannock River, ending the offensive that never really got underway. Jackson's twilight attack on May 2 fell on Salm's former comrades in the XI Corps, which shattered under the pressure. The XI Corps's heavy German makeup made it an ideal scapegoat, an indictment exacerbated by reports that the "Dutchmen" ran. Under the circumstances it was a largely unfair charge, but the stigma remained. German troops would be considered suspect in many minds for the balance of the war. May of 1863 could not have been a worse time for a German to seek a command.[1]

Far away from the field of battle in New York the royal couple took up residence in a most unlikely place—the home of a Methodist minister—and began their search for new employment. The evangelical spirit of the preacher's prayer meetings offered a spectacle that the Salm-Salms found disconcerting. Agnes recalled, "We afterwards always went out on those evenings." Religious fervor was the least of their problems. Salm's early efforts to garner a new commission apparently focused not on acquiring another regiment but on raising a whole brigade. Whether working under a vainglorious miscalculation or prodded by Agnes to achieve bigger things, Salm stood little chance of raising a regiment, let alone a brigade. Nonetheless, he opened a recruiting office in a hotel on lower Broadway, but it would be more than a year before Salm could take the field again.[2]

Agnes and Salm found New York a changed place. The city's enthusiasm for the war had diminished since their last visit, and at Albany, Democrat Horatio Seymour now occupied the governor's office. The war continued to go badly, at that. News from Virginia dashed the high hopes of spring and brought the ugly realization that much more fighting and dying would be required. This, of course, meant that more soldiers were needed, but volunteering had all but stopped. Throughout the North, and especially in New York, federally mandated conscription fomented serious resentment and threatened worse. May and June passed without much outward expression of these feelings, as Governor Seymour vowed to oppose the draft.

So while Salm toiled without result, Agnes pursued more pleasant diversions. She had a busy summer. According to her memoir, she accepted fallen General Blenker's invitation to visit his farm in Rockland County, New York, not far from the United States Military Academy at West Point. "It was a delightful time," she recalled. Back in New York City by July, she found herself in position to witness one of the ugliest expressions of war on the home front—the New York draft riots of 1863.[3]

In late June news that General Lee had once again pointed his army northward spread alarm throughout the New York area. After all, New York was not that far from the Mason-Dixon line, and with only a battered and demoralized Army of the Potomac between Lee's host and America's greatest city, the prospect of invasion became all too real. General Hooker had been replaced, and once again the Army of the Potomac was in disarray. But during the first week of July, Hooker's replacement, Major General George Gordon Meade, made an improbable yet victorious debut when his army withstood three days of desperate attacks by Lee's Confederates at Gettysburg and turned the tide of war in the East for good. The great Federal victory in Pennsylvania, though, was not without negative consequences for the North. Horrendous casualties, including heavy losses in New York units, meant no relief from the impending draft.

The Enrollment Act of March, 1863, mandated that states must draft men from their various militia units and other previously exempt pools to meet quotas left unfilled by volunteers. Although Governor Seymour challenged the constitutionality of the act, the state on July 11 drew the first names. Two days later violence erupted. Most of the Federal troops stationed at New York had been called south to help confront the Confederate invasion, leaving the city in no shape to handle the crisis. The rioters, mostly the city's working men and women, lashed out at all points of wealth and government. What began as a draft protest became an attack on widespread federal intervention, the rich, Republicans, abolitionists, and African Americans. Ironworkers, longshoremen, public works employees, and volunteer firefighters, among others, took out frustrations that had little to do with the draft. For more than four days the city endured a state of war. The majority of rioters were Irish or Irish-American, but Germans, and other emigrant groups, as well as Anglo-American Protestants joined in.[4]

In some of her most lucid and revealing prose, Agnes described the riot and offered her commentary, comparing the event to the "reign of the Commune in Paris." She wrote that Salm offered his services to the city government, collected some troops, and "led them against the rioters." Not content to wait out the horror at home, Agnes claimed, "I wanted to see and to do—but what, I did not know." But she would not do it as a princess: "To go in the street in my usual dress would have been madness, and I resolved therefore to put on a dress of my servant girl, Ellen, who was to accompany me as a kind of safeguard, for she was an Irish girl, and her brogue was then the best *laisser-passer.*" She recorded the many attacks on black men and their families, the burning of a black orphanage, and the total lack of control that existed. She also described the savage killing of Colonel Henry O'Brien, who was beaten to a pulp before being shot through the head—his crime being that he was a soldier and tried to persuade his fellow Irishmen to stop their rampage.[5]

Agnes left no ambiguity in her indictment of the Irish of New York City:

> I have not seen the Irish at home, and cannot judge about them in general. I have become acquainted with well-educated Irish gentlemen and ladies, and found them most intelligent and highly agreeable people, but the low Irish rabble of New York are the most degraded and brutish set of human beings I know; I shudder to think of them, and in my opinion they stand far beneath the negroes. They may, in many respects, be more highly gifted and talented than those, but their behaviour is always meaner and rougher; and the negroes have besides the great advantage over the Irish, that they are sober; a drunken negro is a rarity, whilst drunkenness is the prevailing state amongst the American descendants of Erin.

The irony in her opinion, tied as she was to the German element in America, spoke to the lack of union in the Union war effort. Similar indictments confronted the Germans and other ethnic groups, yet the Irish and the Germans, and indeed the African Americans, proved absolutely essential to the preservation of the United States, a nation that in general terms held them in low regard, as they did each other.[6]

The riot's bloody conclusion did nothing to improve Salm's situation. Responding to pleas from New York's mayor and other prominent citizens, Secretary of War Stanton dispatched newly available soldiers from the triumphant Army of the Potomac, who finally and brutally put down the revolt. For a would-be commander in search of troops, New York could not have been a less fertile recruiting ground. To make matters worse for Salm, reports of the Battle of Gettysburg revealed that once again the XI Corps took a pounding, and the reputation of German troops fell precipitously. By fall, the largely Teutonic XI and XII Corps would be shipped to the Western Theater of operations—to Tennessee. Worse still, Salm's chief supporters in the army had fallen from grace: Hooker never again enjoyed the confidence of Lincoln and would join the XI and XII Corps in Tennessee; and Sickles, whose blundering deployment of his III Corps at Gettysburg threatened disaster, had lost a leg in the battle, removing him from any important role in the army.[7]

While Salm continued his recruiting efforts, to little avail, Agnes went about the cultivation of new influential friends. Her efforts proved more productive than those of her husband; in fact, she pulled off something of a coup. James Gordon Bennett, the Scotland-born publisher of one of America's leading newspapers, the *New York Herald,* was among the most powerful men in the country. Agnes's friendship with the Bennett family was as improbable as the rest of her career. He was staunchly anti-abolitionist, anti-Catholic, anti-aristocrat, and could be anti-foreign, as well as mostly anti-Republican. Yet Bennett supported Lincoln and the war effort, and in so doing developed an interesting relationship with the president. Agnes recalled the hospitality that Bennett and his family extended during her stay in New York. "I was a frequent guest at his magnificent country-seat at Port Washington, and at his palatial mansion on the Fifth Avenue," she wrote, adding that he was "a very good man, and extremely kind to us."

More compelling, perhaps, was her relationship with James G. Bennett, Jr., who at roughly her age represented an opportunity for the kind of sexual adventurism with which she was often associated, although no hint of such ever surfaced. A nineteenth-century millionaire playboy-sportsman, the younger Bennett would inherit his father's publishing empire and attract international renown in 1870, when he sent correspondent Henry Morgan Stanley to Africa to find explorer Dr. David Livingstone. On one of Agnes's visits to Port Washington, "Mr. James" presented her with a "pup of a particularly fine breed, a black and tan long-legged terrier" from his "live museum" of dogs. She named the dog Jimmy, and with Salm's help she raised the pup on fried oysters and hard-boiled egg yolks until he grew old enough for roast veal, which became his favorite food. Jimmy the terrier would be Agnes's near-constant companion for many years and through much adventure.[8]

The connection with the Bennetts became much more than a casual association, and not only for Agnes. In October, the senior Bennett wrote to President Lincoln on various war-related issues and requested the president's consideration of an enclosed letter from Mrs. Bennett, asking for Salm a brigadier general's commission. Such endorsements could not hurt, but in this case the request went unfulfilled.[9]

For what she described as a "rather troublesome sojourn in New York," Agnes appeared to have had a pretty good time. In addition to her pleasant trip to Blenker's farm and her visits to the Bennett properties, not to mention her draft riot adventures, Agnes found time to dabble in the spiritualist movement that then swept much of the country.

The practice of communicating with the dead—spirits—through a medium became one manifestation of the religious revivalism the country had experienced. Spiritualism likely began in Europe in the early nineteenth century and found its greatest expression in America with the Fox sisters, Kate and Margaret, who attracted international notice in the 1850s. In 1863 spiritualism attracted Agnes.[10] Her interest appeared to stem more out of a sense of mischief than genuine curiosity. Although she "resisted this epidemic on the ground of religion and common sense," she could not avoid "becoming interested in this strange aberration, and feeling tempted to witness some manifestations of spiritualism." The prince, she noted, admonished her to refrain, as he believed that the experience might "act too strongly on my imagination." He may have been correct. Agnes devoted more than eight pages to this diversion in her memoir—a good deal more than she reserved for other such ancillary topics. But Salm had the last laugh. After joining Agnes for a presentation, during which a female medium made a piano move, Salm pronounced that he too was a medium. "He sat down, and after having run over the keys," Agnes recalled, "the piano moved in the same manner as before. He had simply pressed his knees under it, and lifted it on one side an inch or two. The detected medium received her five dollars, and retired somewhat confused."[11]

Sometime in the fall of 1863 Governor Seymour offered Salm the command of another regiment, but the offer evidently came with the proviso that the unit must be brought up to strength before Salm could muster in as its colonel. The 68th New York Infantry was an active regiment but one much depleted by casualties, sickness, and other causes after two years in the field. It had fought in the Shenandoah Valley, at Second Bull Run, and at Fredericksburg; it suffered with the XI Corps at Chancellorsville and Gettysburg, and with the rest of the corps had moved on to Tennessee. Its colonel, Gotthiff Bourry, had left the regiment before its transfer west, and Lieutenant Colonel Albert von Steinhausen now headed the regiment. Like most Union regiments, the 68th was a three-year regiment, its enlistment scheduled to expire in August, 1864. Without substantial reenlistments and an influx of new soldiers, the 68th would cease to exist as a complete regiment.[12]

Salm might have a regiment, but he still had to fill its ranks before it meant anything. His recruiting efforts, however, stalled. Now Agnes rose to the challenge. She contacted "dear old" Senator Harris, who suggested that the provost marshal general in Washington might have unassigned troops available. Without disclosing the nature of her journey she traveled to the capital on the pretext of visiting her sister. In Washington, she immediately called on Provost Marshal General Colonel James B. Fry. For some unexplained reason, "It was some comfort" to her that he was "a married man." A handsome and highly efficient career staff officer, Fry administered a department charged with conscription enforcement, desertion control, and the organization of unassigned recruits. According to Agnes, he agreed to detail the "few hundred" men he had at his disposal to the 68th New York. Never one for modesty, she wrote: "I was overjoyed at my success."[13]

Still short of her goal, she persuaded Fry to help raise the rest. To that end he introduced her to Illinois Governor Richard Yates. The Republican Yates, like New York's Morgan, wielded substantial power and like Morgan raised impressively large numbers of troops for the Union. "Having occasion to confer frequently with [Colonel] Fry and Governor Yates," Agnes recalled, "we became good friends and I passed many agreeable hours in the company of these distinguished men."

While in Washington Agnes moved about the city's transient society and frequented centers of power such as Willard's Hotel, with the provost marshal general as her guide. "Colonel Fry was very kind in this respect," and at length interested Governor Yates in Agnes's mission. According to Agnes, Yates offered a company of Illinois troops but refused to have it commanded by a New York officer. To prevent this, she wrote, "I received from him a captain's commission and captain's pay, which, he said, would assist me in defraying the expenses I incurred in assisting the sick and wounded soldiers, in whose treatment I was much interested." With that she became the Soldier Princess of legend, although Yates left no record of the "commission."[14]

Other women apparently received state-issued commissions during the war (the United States did not commission women), and thousands of women on both sides pressed the interests of husbands, brothers, and sons to government officials. Reportedly, Governor Yates also

commissioned one Belle Reynolds a major for her service to wounded
Illinois troops. Madame Nadine Turchin, wife of Russia-born Brigadier
General John Turchin, actually led her husband's Illinois regiment for
several days. Fanny Gordon, wife of Confederate hero Major General
John B. Gordon, nursed wounded soldiers and zealously promoted her
husband's interests. And Jessie Benton Frémont, wife of ill-fated Federal General John C. Frémont and daughter of powerful Senator
Thomas Hart Benton, exceeded even Agnes in her determined efforts
on her husband's behalf, once tearing into Lincoln for relieving the
ineffectual general.[15]

The petty pursuits of Agnes Salm-Salm and Jessie Frémont and
dozens like them could not diminish the profound impact that women
had on all facets of the war. Women left their traditional roles by the
thousands to tend to the wounded or support relief organizations near
the front, while thousands more tended to family farms or worked in
war-related industries. Others performed as spies. And yes, many women
fought, often disguised as men. Some women won accolades for their
contributions, and one, a surgeon named Mary Edwards Walker received the Medal of Honor. But for most women, the Civil War brought
hardship, and in the end failed substantially to alter their situations
once peace returned. The access and attention enjoyed by Agnes and
Jessie Frémont came more as products of privilege than from the recognition of merit.[16]

Agnes likely did receive some kind of unofficial commission from
Yates, and certainly the pay would have been welcomed, whether or not
she used any money she may have received for the care of the sick and
wounded. Interestingly, the reference to sick and wounded soldiers in
connection to her dealings with Governor Yates marked the first time
that this aspect of her career—for which she was most acknowledged—
appeared in her memoir, and it came two years into her wartime experience. Prior to this time she evidenced no such interest. Nor was she
involved in the Sanitary Commission or other related efforts. But from
this time on Agnes grew increasingly interested in such matters, an
interest that would reach fruition during the Franco-Prussian War.

Thanks to Agnes's recruiting efforts, Salm's regiment began to take
shape. But while she worked in Washington and Salm labored, without
much success, in New York, the 68th New York Volunteer Infantry under
Lieutenant Colonel Steinhausen earned some much-needed redemption

at Chattanooga. In October and November, 1863, as part of a demi-army comprised of the XI and XII Corps commanded by General Hooker, the 68th took part in the relief of the important Tennessee railroad center, and then shared in one of the most important Union victories of the war as Major General U. S. Grant's Federal troops swept General Braxton Bragg's Confederates off Lookout Mountain and Missionary Ridge.

Concerned that three-year enlistments would run out during the height of expected summer fighting in 1864 and well aware that volunteering had dried up, the government approached old regiments with new inducements to reenlist, including state and federal bounties that could amount to $700 and a month of furlough. The idea was to get regiments to reenlist *en masse,* and if seventy-five percent of the existing regiment did so it could retain its numerical designation, its flag, and its organization. The regiment would receive Veteran Volunteer status, and its soldiers could wear a service stripe to indicate a second enlistment. This would give Salm something to build on, and once Agnes's acquisitions fell in, the regiment would be formed. But that would take time. The veterans of the 68th reenlisted in December, and on January 12, 1864, they left Chattanooga for New York and a well-deserved furlough. They returned to Tennessee in March with Steinhausen still in command. Assigned to the Fourth Division of General Hooker's new XX Corps, Army of the Cumberland, the 68th took station at Bridgeport, Alabama, in April, mustering an aggregate total of 334 men (the number present for duty was likely less than half that).[17]

It was not until June 8 that Salm mustered back into service at Nashville. His new regiment had filled out with a company from the old 8th New York and, presumably, with some of the troops promised to Agnes in Washington. But according to one veteran of the 68th, the holdovers were none too happy about their new colonel. Captain Frederick Otto von Fritsch related that he, Steinhausen, and another officer used part of their veteran furlough to travel to Albany to protest Salm's appointment. They had hoped, with justification, to move up the regimental ladder in reorganization, but they came too late. The colonelcy had long since been awarded, and Fritsch thought he knew why: "[Salm's] beautiful wife had done the talking—and a good deal of smiling and coaxing." So, as they had been with the 8th, the Salm-Salms would be outsiders, already unwanted by the new regiment's officers and men.[18]

Agnes waited in Washington until Salm got settled with his new command. From Nashville, the colonel moved to Bridgeport, where the 68th had established its camp. Although far removed from the major events of the war, the regiment belonged to General Sherman's Military Division of the Mississippi, the bulk of which had pushed to the outskirts of Atlanta by July, 1864. But to sustain his campaign against Atlanta, Sherman depended on a tenuous rail link that stretched all the way to Nashville and on to Louisville. Maintenance of this vital connection required dozens of units posted at strategic points along the Nashville & Chattanooga Railroad to guard against Confederate raiders, namely the dreaded Nathan Bedford Forrest. At Bridgeport, in the far northeastern corner of Alabama, the 68th New York guarded the railroad where it crossed the mighty Tennessee River. It was an unglamorous assignment shared by the thousands of troops who supported Sherman's main effort in Georgia.[19]

In July, Agnes, accompanied by a maid and her faithful dog Jimmy, headed to Nashville, but circumstances—the war—prevented her from moving on to Bridgeport. As fighting heated up in Atlanta, Salm managed to pay her an eight-day visit, "riding all the way on horseback." She begged to return with him to Alabama, but Salm talked her out of it. "The guerrillas were very ferocious," she wrote, "and I really believe that my being a lady would not have protected me against their outrages." He asked her to return to Washington until he could bring her safely to Bridgeport. She did as requested. Nashville held no charms for her, anyway.[20]

While Agnes waited, Salm and his new regiment got to know each other. Fritsch, a German nobleman himself, leveled some caustic allegations against his colonel, charges not altogether improbable. He claimed that Salm brought with him seven men to whom he had promised commissions in exchange for their past financial support, and that the colonel attempted to run off existing officers to make room for his cronies. Captain Fritsch also revived the familiar indictment of the cash-strapped prince: "Like all such men, he would have been a perfect gentleman and a most charming companion if possessed of sufficient means, but situated as he was, he did many things which he would not have done had he been well off." But then Fritsch and the officers held a considerable grudge.[21]

Fritsch was yet to meet Agnes, but she was on the way. Salm picked a strange time to deem it safe for her return to the Western Theater. After finally yielding Atlanta on September 1, Confederate General John Bell Hood soon headed his army north and then westward into Alabama in preparation for a march on Nashville. This put the Bridgeport garrison in a potentially vulnerable situation. Still, Agnes, accompanied by Madame Corvin and Jimmy, left Washington on October 1. Madame Corvin, the wife of Salm's comrade, found that American trains, especially the sleeping cars, compared quite favorably to those of Europe. They traveled to Pittsburgh, which reminded Madame Corvin of Manchester, England, then to Louisville, and on to Nashville. At the Tennessee capital, they found their further transit forbidden because of heightened military activity to the south. "I fortunately discovered some officers who knew me," Agnes wrote, and they "smuggled us into the last of the cars." The twenty-four-hour ride on a military train was, she believed, "the most fatiguing and disagreeable journey I ever made."[22]

Indeed, it must have been a harrowing time. As if rough terrain, signs of wrecked locomotives and rolling stock, and the persistent threat of guerrilla attack were not enough, Agnes confronted "a calamity worse than the rebels." Jimmy the dog jumped train. As further evidence that Agnes never much understood the gravity of the greater event in which she participated, she confessed that she pulled the emergency cord and brought the train to a halt. The captain in charge somehow managed to control himself and allowed Jimmy to reboard.[23]

Agnes found Salm's command stationed on a large, flood-prone island in the Tennessee River near Bridgeport. If Salm stirred negative feelings in the regiment, the princess had the opposite effect. Captain Fritsch recalled fondly his first meeting: "She then shook hands with me and gave me one of the most charming, bewildering of smiles, with which she conquered all men, and I deeply regretted that she did not add an embrace and a kiss besides." Fritsch also offered a most insightful description. "Besides her great beauty, the Princess was known for her remarkably free and easy manners, her determined ways and daring horsemanship, and of course other ladies considered her a mere adventuress; but in reality she was only a very shrewd woman, whose motto was the same as that of the Jesuits: 'The end justifies the means.'" He continued, "She was never vulgar, but blushed easily, and often showed that at heart she was a most respectable little woman. Naturally, she made use of her charms, and bestowed her favors on those who could promote her husband's interests. Proud and politely cold with ordinary men, she was seductive only with influential people and a few personal friends." Strangely, Agnes made no mention of Fritsch.[24]

As Bridgeport offered little opportunity to woo influential people, Agnes turned her energies to her professed passion—the care of sick and wounded soldiers. During her stay on the island and in nearby Bridgeport she worked to improve conditions at local hospitals, often traveling to Nashville or Chattanooga to gather supplies. She did not nurse the men nor did she, as was often reported, tend the wounded on the battlefield but acted rather as benefactor, using her title and tenacity to acquire what normal channels failed to provide. It was the beginning of a new career.[25]

The Alabama posting was not without diversions. In one instance Captain Fritsch conducted a "sham defense" of a blockhouse for invited guests in honor of Agnes. In late October the Salm-Salms accepted Major General James Steedman's invitation to visit Chattanooga, just a breathtaking train ride to the east. There they toured many sites of the great Union victory less than a year before and made a special day trip up Lookout Mountain. "After having feasted our eyes to our hearts' content," Agnes recalled, they shared an "exquisite breakfast which General Steedman had sent up, together with a good supply of champagne, which made us all very merry."[26]

But there was a war going on, and November brought some anxiety for the soldiers of Major General George Thomas's Army of the Cumberland. After crossing the Tennessee River at Tuscumbia, Alabama, General Hood marched his battered Confederate army northward and into Tennessee. Hood's goal had been to draw Sherman's army out of Georgia while he pushed on to Nashville, Louisville, and the Ohio River. But on November 15, Sherman turned his back on Hood and began his "March to the Sea," leaving Thomas to deal with the threat. Thomas was plenty capable of dealing with Hood, but the bold move sent a low-key panic through the North. In bad weather the Confederates pressed northward, driving Federal forces from Columbia and almost isolating a sizable command at Spring Hill. At Franklin on November 30, Hood attacked Major General John Schofield's army and suffered terrible casualties, but he pushed on toward Nashville, only a few miles distant. Thomas now called in his far-flung army for a final showdown.

In December the prince finally received a chance to participate in a major campaign. General Steedman, who now commanded the District of the Etowah, received orders to form a provisional detachment from his district and rush with it to Nashville. While the 68th was not among the troops assembled for the emergency, Steedman detailed Salm to his provisional staff. On December 15 and 16, after much prodding, the deliberate Thomas and his amalgamated force destroyed Hood's army on the frozen hills of Nashville. Salm's efforts during the battle went unrecorded, but he commanded a provisional brigade in the pursuit of the retreating Confederates. The pursuit lasted into January, 1865, and stretched back to Alabama. In his report on the Nashville Campaign, General Steedman wrote that Salm "exhibited high qualities as a soldier" in recommending him for promotion.[27]

Agnes had curious memories of the time when Salm was away fighting. Again, she appeared to have not the slightest interest in the serious events that surrounded her. As Salm prepared to ship out for Nashville, she passed the time "eating and drinking Catawba champagne," and expressed indignation that the events prevented her planned trip to Washington. And while her husband risked his life she entertained Brigadier General Robert S. Granger, commanding the District of Northern Alabama, and Brigadier General John Brannan, Army of the Cumberland chief of artillery, then on an inspection tour of the department. She recalled that General Granger, whom she called a *bon-vivant*, invited her to nearby Stevenson for fine music and "exquisite dinners." Transportation was no problem. "Whenever we wanted to make such an excursion," she wrote, "I telegraphed my old friend General [Thomas] Meagher, commanding then in Chattanooga, to send me a locomotive, which he never failed to do, in spite of the grumbling of the officers in charge of the railroad department." To Agnes, apparently, the army was hers for the using.[28]

After a brief rendezvous with Salm at Stevenson, Agnes returned to Bridgeport, where she celebrated Christmas with Mrs. Corvin and her husband, who had joined them for the winter. They had a "nice time," she recalled, "and we were as happy as could be." With the railroad again open, Agnes and the Corvins in early January started for Washington, but at Nashville, the princess received word of Salm's return to Bridgeport, so she resolved to return as well.[29]

CHAPTER 3

General Felix Salm

On January 14 Salm assumed command of the post at Bridgeport, but now that he had gotten into the war he would not be a mere garrison officer. Throughout the winter and into spring he led his brigade against isolated Rebel detachments and guerrilla bands in Tennessee, Alabama, and Georgia, fighting small engagements at places like Elrod's Tanyard, Hog Jaw Valley, and Johnson's Crook. Salm led most of these raids in person and acquitted himself well in many minor actions.[1]

Meanwhile, Agnes wasted no time in relocating their things to the post commander's quarters in Bridgeport proper—off the island on the bluff overlooking the river. February brought the arrival of her sister Della and her husband Edmund Johnson, and at least one son. Perhaps a manifestation of the paternalism that Fritsch criticized, in this case nepotism, Johnson moved from civil life into the captaincy of Company E, 68th New York, and was quickly detailed to Salm's brigade staff. But the reunion failed to quench Agnes's thirst for bigger things.[2]

General Steedman had recommended Salm's promotion, but, as winter passed, the prince remained a colonel. The subject became a cause unto itself for Agnes. "After due reflection," she wrote, "it was thought best that I . . . should go to Washington and look after the interests of Felix and his brigade." She always saw things through the eyes of a princess: "To Europeans, especially to Germans, this meddling of ladies, especially with military affairs, will appear rather strange, but every country has its peculiarities, and it is one of the peculiarities of America that ladies have there a far different position from that they hold in Europe. More things go through their hands than outsiders dream of, and officials in different bureaus are not in the least surprised if ladies attend to the business of their husbands."

Most nineteenth-century American women, and men for that matter, would take exception to this assertion; Agnes, though, tended to accept her experience as the general condition. But Captain Fritsch recognized her as unique and was quite willing to profit from her exertions. He maintained that she promised to work for his promotion to colonel of the 68th, once Salm received his generalship, quoting her: "I invariably succeed when I put my war paint on." He would be disappointed. On February 24, 1865, Agnes left for the East to secure for her husband his coveted brigadier's star—with no doubt whatsoever that Salm fully deserved the promotion.[3]

In light of Salm's relative lack of wartime activity, the quest for his promotion would have been preposterous had the Civil War not produced such a deflation of the general's grade. In the Federal army almost 600 men became general officers of full rank during the war, many with even less legitimate claims than Salm's. Throughout the Civil War the United States operated two major military establishments. The Regular Army consisted of the extant prewar regiments and even after a sizable expansion had an authorized strength of only 42,000, which it never reached. For the war, though, the government established the United States Volunteers, which constituted the main fighting force and numbered at war's end more than a million men. Of the Union's 583 general officers only 11 held the grade in the regular establishment; of the rest, only 194 were professional soldiers. Because Lincoln's prosecution of the war depended on political support, dozens of men whose best claim to military command was their ability to provide that support or to enlist large numbers of their constituents became colonels and generals, a good many commanded corps and some even armies. Dozens of Regular Army officers took leaves to accept higher grades in the Volunteers—a practice supported by the government. As the war drew to a close hundreds of officers lobbied to pad their résumés. Salm's claim, while highly dubious, was not all that out of line. Still, others, more deserving but lacking important sponsorship, went unrecognized.[4]

Agnes proved to be a capable sponsor, but she too needed political backing. In Washington she pulled every string she had. At the War Department she saw General Hooker and her old ally, James Fry, now a brigadier general, who kept her posted on the department's activities, but they had little to offer. The Senate had to confirm all general officers based on recommendations from Secretary of War Stanton. And Stanton was one man in Washington who refused to see Agnes. She called on Senator Harris and Richard Yates, who had only recently taken a seat in the Senate. Yates promised his help, but Agnes, leaving nothing to chance, left for New York to lobby Governor Reuben Fenton. She also sought the assistance of New Hampshire Governor Joseph Gilmore. Both men vowed to support Salm's promotion. Agnes's machinations, as it turned out, meant nothing because General Thomas had not forwarded a recommendation.[5]

Thoroughly exhausted, Agnes returned to Washington, where she rested at the Corvins' home in Georgetown. True to his word, Senator Yates did what he could. He wired General Thomas at Nashville: "Genl Steedman has telegraphed strong recommendations for promotion of Col Salm of the Sixty-Eighth NY will you also telegraph the Secy of War a recommendation in his favor." Thomas complied. Yates informed Agnes that he would see Stanton on April 12, and when she called on him the next day Yates presented her with Salm's brevet to brigadier general of U.S. Volunteers for "meritorious services" in the Nashville Campaign. She immediately sent to Bridgeport a telegraph "addressed to *General* Felix Salm." But this was her triumph: "Yes, I felt extremely happy and proud. He had given me his name and made me a princess, but notwithstanding his name and rank he would have failed after his first start, and remained a colonel without a regiment, involved as he was in the fate of poor Blenker. All his merit would have availed him little against the rancour of Stanton. I procured for him the command of the 8th, and raised for him the 68th Regiment; now he had become a general through my exertions."

Correct as she may have been, this lack of modesty lent credibility to her critics' comments, going all the way back to the aggrieved officers of the 8th, who found her boasts most offensive—not to mention in poor taste.[6]

Agnes need not have been so pleased with herself; in reality she had accomplished very little. Brevet ranks were conferred much like decorations for gallantry, war service, and in some cases for no apparent reason. More than 1,300 officers became generals by brevet only, never gaining the substantive or full rank, which was what Agnes sought. An officer could command at his brevet rank when so directed on a temporary basis (for example, when a commanding general wanted a junior colonel to command a brigade over a more senior colonel, the junior officer could command at his brevet rank). What these brevets meant more than anything else was that another 1,300 men could call themselves "generals." Agnes might call him a general and he might command as a general, but Salm remained colonel of the 68th New York for the rest of the war. The diminished nature of Salm's promotion failed to register on her.[7]

But then, she could count herself lucky to have gotten anything. The week of April 9 began with news of Robert E. Lee's surrender to General Grant at Appomattox Court House; three days later Mobile fell to Federal forces. On the thirteenth, the same day he issued Salm's brevet, Stanton halted the draft and began the long process of demobilization. The long war was almost over. On Good Friday, April 14, President Lincoln went to the theater.[8]

Still in Washington on the morning of April 15, Agnes learned of Lincoln's assassination by John Wilkes Booth. (In her memoir she referred to the killer once as William Booth and once as Edwin Booth.) "Though I mourned very much the death of the good and kind President," she wrote, "war had hardened me somewhat against the impression of such scenes and news, and I left the same evening for New York to attend to my private business." Private business in this case meant that she had to order a general's uniform for Salm. That done, she returned to Washington on the nineteenth—the day of Lincoln's funeral. Over the next few days, she attended to various concerns and, never one to bypass an opportunity to make powerful friends, gained an audience with new President Andrew Johnson. In May she headed westward to join her husband, now stationed at Dalton, Georgia. She rode the last leg, from Chattanooga to Dalton, on a locomotive's cow-catcher. But as the war wound down, things remained interesting for the princess.[9]

Agnes related a strange story from that spring. According to the princess, her eighteen-year-old sister Della, whose husband had been detailed as ordnance officer to the post of Cleveland, Tennessee, ex-pected her second child in July. "I felt very envious," Agnes recalled, "for I had no child, which made me quite unhappy." Curiously, Della offered the new child to Agnes, "should it be a boy." Good as her word, upon giving birth, Della presented to her sister a baby boy, whom Agnes named Felix: "I was extremely happy to have at last a baby, and it be-came the centre around which everything turned—even my pet Jimmy was neglected. Little Felix was a most beautiful child, the black nurse felt very proud, as black nurses of white children always do. It was quite amusing to hear her breaking out in ecstasies about her nursling, and preferring him much to her own child, which she contemptuously called a black brat."

It was so like Agnes. She had gone through a war as if it were staged for her amusement and now she had a child without the rigors of child-birth. The peculiar arrangement proved short-lived, though, as the child would not take to the nurse and had to be returned to his mother.[10]

The war, meanwhile, moved steadily toward its conclusion. In late April, Confederate General Joseph Johnston surrendered his army to General Sherman in North Carolina; on May 10 President Jefferson Davis was captured in Georgia; and later that month at New Orleans, Lieutenant General Simon Bolivar Buckner surrendered the Trans-Mississippi Department—the last major Confederate organization. In July, Salm's Second Brigade, Second Separate Division, Army of the Cumberland, moved on to the devastated city of Atlanta. In November, 1864, Sherman's men had destroyed what remained of the railroad cen-ter after its surrender, leaving behind a pile of rubble and twisted rails as they marched on toward Savannah and the sea.

The Salm-Salms found a desolate place and an impoverished people. Salm, as acting military governor of the area, had a tough job. He "tried his best to restore confidence in the district, and to check the insolence of the soldiery." Through his humanitarian efforts and Agnes's work in local hospitals, "going now and then to Augusta, or even to Nashville, to fetch provisions," they managed, according to Agnes, to earn some public appreciation, although Atlantans would have been hard-pressed to appreciate any man in a blue uniform.[11]

The family was not without difficulties. Captain Johnson, who came to Atlanta as Salm's provost marshal, was charged with misappropriation of funds, but an inquiry cleared him of all charges. Johnson and Della then moved on to Augusta, where he served as assistant provost marshal general for the department. Still, as Agnes recalled, "time passed agreeably well with us."[12]

The demobilization of the massive Federal army progressed through the summer and into fall as Volunteer regiments gradually mustered out of service. In October, Salm received orders to proceed with his regiment to Savannah. Agnes joined Della in Augusta to await further instructions. There she looked in on the hospitals but mostly dashed about on a locomotive in search of supplies, riding again on the cowcatcher. "This manner of travelling is not at all disagreeable, for one has fresh air, and is free from the dust and heat of the locomotive." Soon she joined Salm and the 68th Regiment at Fort Pulaski, the heavily damaged bastion on the Atlantic coast near Savannah.[13]

Captain Fritsch, whose literary flights of fancy rivaled those of Agnes, maintained that Salm had gone to Savannah under arrest for "some deeds of doubtful character," upon which he refused to elaborate because of the "horror of European noblemen disgracing themselves." He claimed that Salm escaped judgment by fleeing to Mexico, "leaving the dear Princess behind," and that he had raised the funds to ship her to Veracruz. Of course, Agnes mentioned nothing of the sort; and Salm's record reflected no malfeasance.[14]

According to Agnes's version of events, she and Salm took a steamer up the Savannah River to Augusta that October to tie up some loose ends. On the way to Augusta their boat ran aground and Salm resisted the urge to track and kill a rather large alligator that he noticed on shore. Transferred to another vessel, they assisted in the rescue of a crew whose supply ship sank in the river. They retrieved besides a "box of fine claret and a basket of champagne" and proceeded to "make acquaintance with the contents of box and basket."[15]

At Augusta, Salm learned that his regiment was to be discharged. He and Agnes rushed back to Fort Pulaski, where on November 30,

1865, the 68th New York (Veteran) Volunteer Infantry mustered out of federal service. The war had long since been over, but now Salm faced unemployment again and his prospects were few and far between. So, as his men boarded a steamer for New York, Salm opted instead to go with his wife to Washington.[16]

Salm was not without opportunities in America. Many volunteer officers from the war found places in the Regular Army, and with Agnes's connections her husband stood a better than average chance of landing a regular commission. But many wartime generals became captains or majors in the postwar establishment, and a peacetime army held little appeal to glory-seeking soldiers. Some of these warriors received offers of employment from Egypt and Turkey and South America. And there was always Mexico. Salm, as Agnes pointed out, "could not fully be reconciled to living [in the United States] for ever" and had hoped to return to Europe—to his family. But "having spent his fortune" and with the loss of his colonel's pay, Salm had to decide soon upon what course he would take. He quickly ruled out the prospect of remaining in the United States, commenting that he was "horrified at the idea of living a dreary life in some little garrison beyond the pale of civilization."[17]

For Salm, there appeared to be a sort of mercenary's integrity. "To speak the truth," he wrote, "I was a soldier with all my soul, and war was my element. What I had seen of it in Europe and America served only to make me more eager to extend my experience, and I resolved to offer my services to the Emperor Maximilian of Mexico, for whose person and civilizing task I had always felt great sympathy." His decision made sense. Maximilian was an Austrian—Salm had served the Austrian Empire as a young soldier and, like most Europeans who knew or heard tale of the affable young Hapsburg duke, he felt a genuine affection. But as far as the United States was concerned, Maximilian represented the enemy.[18]

CHAPTER 4

Like a Female Centaur

It was rather like the Prince and Princess Salm-Salm to jump from one adventure to another. Never ones to dwell on the past or wait too long for the future to take shape, they proceeded to the next attraction with clear determination. On December 10 they boarded a Baltimore-bound steamer at Savannah. After a rough passage, they arrived at the Chesapeake port city, where they caught a train for Washington. Back in the familiar capital, they visited friends and began to accumulate letters of recommendation and introductions to the Imperial Court of Mexico. Salm secured promises of favorable endorsements from the ambassadors of Prussia, Austria, and France. Both he and Agnes insisted that President Andrew Johnson, although he could not provide official letters of introduction, supported the idea and gave Salm a "very flattering testimony."

With everything in apparent readiness, they moved on to New York. They decided that Agnes should stay with the Corvins in Georgetown until Salm established himself in Mexico and could call her to join him.

Imperial Mexico would be more his milieu, anyway. So in late February, Salm, accompanied by his aide-de-camp, sailed for Veracruz.[1]

Perhaps Prince Felix could have made a worse decision than to offer his sword to Maximilian, but it would have taken some doing. Mexico was, when Salm arrived in March, 1866, a particularly bad place to be for any European prince—and for good reason.

Mexico had been at war with itself for much of its existence. In the time since they won their independence from Spain in 1821, Mexicans had suffered a series of internal battles for political control, the embarrassing loss of Texas, and the humiliating invasion by the United States that took away another huge chunk of their land. In the 1855 Revolution of Ayutla, Mexican liberals wrested control of the country from the ubiquitous Antonio López de Santa Anna. The liberals brought a reform agenda that lashed out at the Roman Catholic Church and a corrupt military establishment. *Ley Juárez,* named for Secretary of Justice Benito Juárez, deprived the Church and the military of civil jurisdiction, while *Ley Lerdo,* after Secretary of Development Miguel Lerdo de Tejada, prohibited the Church or the government from owning property not directly associated with their immediate operations. For the property-rich Church, Ley Lerdo dealt a severe blow. *La Reforma,* the Reform, as the era came to be known, hit hard at Mexican conservatives and created a formidable enemy in Rome. The liberal Constitution of 1857 struck even deeper, officially abolishing slavery, titles of nobility, and guaranteeing habeas corpus among other basic rights.[2]

Conservatives battled back. In the War of the Reform (from 1858 to 1861), Mexicans again fought among themselves. It became a bitter and brutal, back-and-forth conflict from which the liberals emerged victorious—with Juárez as president. But the conservatives and the Church plotted a return. The liberal victory left traditional ailments unhealed. There remained a gulf between the Indians and *mestizos* (Mexicans of mixed Indian and Spanish blood) on the one hand, and creoles (Mexicans born of pure Spanish blood). And while the creoles made up the bulk of the elite class, Indians and mestizos by no means flocked *en masse* to the liberals, although Juárez and other prominent Indians made considerable leaps to the forefront. The majority of Mexicans found their lives little if any improved.

Liberal leaders confronted internal differences and fiscal problems of mammoth proportions. They split over the treatment of the defeated conservatives. A sizable contingent of radicals demanded retribution, including the severe punishment—or executions—of conservative leaders. Juárez opted for a more enlightened approach—a wide-ranging amnesty—in hopes of returning Mexico to political and economic viability. Juárez won out, but he would have reason to regret his magnanimity. At the bottom line, though, forty years of internal strife and the resultant lack of development left Mexico with a massive domestic and foreign debt that the troubled republic simply could not bear. Mexico could not move forward until the debt crisis found resolution.

In 1861, as Felix Salm-Salm left Europe to avoid his creditors, Mexico dealt with its own credit problems. President Benito Juárez issued a proclamation that, like his lenient treatment of his enemies, brought far-reaching consequences. He suspended Mexico's debt payments for a period of two years. Representatives from Great Britain, Spain, and France met in London that October and signed a pact by which the three powers would occupy Mexico's primary port of Veracruz in order to collect the outstanding sums. But the Convention of London maintained that the European powers would not use the opportunity to advance territorial designs or to interfere with Mexico's internal operations. By December, 1861, representative forces from the three powers had taken station at Veracruz. While Spain and Britain appeared prepared to honor the tenets of the convention, France had other plans.[3]

Since the Seven Years' War (1756–63) virtually deprived France of a North American presence, France had thirsted to reestablish itself in the Western Hemisphere. Emperor Napoleon III, nephew of Napoleon Bonaparte, since coming to power in 1848, had tried to duplicate his uncle's imperial reach, moving into Indochina and strengthening the French presence in Africa and the Middle East. Mexico's internal chaos opened the door to French conquest. Spain and Britain cut satisfactory deals with the Juárez government and left Mexico in early 1862, but France reinforced its contingent and moved inland. On May 5, *Cinco de Mayo*, a ragtag Mexican army repulsed the pride of Europe at Puebla. But a year later the French took Puebla and marched into Mexico City, beginning their intervention in earnest.

Napoleon, with the forceful backing of his able wife Empress Eugénie, planned to install a European monarch on a French-supported throne in Mexico. He surveyed Europe for a suitable candidate. He settled upon and then cultivated the Austrian Archduke Ferdinand Maximilian von Hapsburg, whose brother Franz Josef ruled the Austrian Empire and headed one of the oldest and most powerful dynastic lines in Europe. While Napoleon hoped to implant a conservative monarch who would rule a Catholic empire in Mexico, the idealistic and well-liked Maximilian held decidedly liberal tendencies and saw in Mexico the potential for a great humanitarian experiment. Maximilian had the additional attribute of a clever, well-born wife—the Belgian Princess Charlotte, who adopted the name Carlota for her role in Mexico. After much coaxing, guarantees of French support (monetary and military), and intense lobbying from Mexican conservatives, the Hapsburg prince accepted Napoleon's offer upon the satisfactory results of a Mexican plebiscite, which conservative leaders easily and fraudulently produced. The thirty-two-year-old archduke and admiral of the Austrian navy prepared for his new life.

Napoleon's American enterprise quickly backfired as Maximilian proved to be anything but the conservative old-world monarch. The Emperor Maximilian and the Empress Carlota arrived at Veracruz in May, 1864. Like most Europeans, and North Americans for that matter, they viewed the Mexicans as a primitive people desperately in need of a civilizing influence. Maximilian, who truly believed that the Mexican people had called him, tried to bring that influence, but at the same time he angered his sponsors—the conservatives and the Church—by not dismantling much of the previous liberal legislation. But he could not elude the fact that he was a European, sent to Mexico to do what the rest of the civilized world believed that Mexicans were incapable of doing for themselves. And this the liberals could not tolerate, nor could any Mexican nationalist—political considerations notwithstanding. So Maximilian quickly found himself without a constituency, bolstered only by French troops and a small Imperial army, consisting of Austrians, Belgians, assorted mercenaries, and some ill-trained and ill-equipped Mexican troops. Against him stood Mexico's legitimate government under Benito Juárez and the Republican army, small though it was, that refused to go away.[4]

Napoleon's initial timing could not have been better. By the time he landed additional troops in Mexico, the United States was well into its own civil war. The insertion of French troops into Mexico for the purpose of overthrowing the legitimate government constituted a serious violation of the Monroe Doctrine, the cornerstone of U.S. foreign policy.

Drafted by Secretary of State John Quincy Adams and issued in 1823 by President James Monroe, the doctrine declared the Western Hemisphere off-limits to further European colonization, that any attempt to extend European political systems to the Americas or to interfere with the free states of the hemisphere would be viewed as an act unfriendly to the United States. For its part, the United States would not interfere with existing colonies or in the internal affairs of Europe. On the surface, the Monroe Doctrine supported the sovereignty of the newly liberated states of Spanish America, including Mexico. But the United States also hoped to exploit the economic void left by Spain's departure. Although for most of the nineteenth century the United States could not enforce the doctrine as such, it became the nation's most cherished piece of foreign policy.[5]

So as Napoleon's intentions became clear in early 1862, the United States was powerless to stop the French. And the French took full advantage of the situation, inserting some 40,000 troops. By the Convention of Miramar, the formal arrangement that brought Maximilian and Carlota to Mexico, Napoleon pledged to maintain a sizable French force in Mexico through 1867, with the Foreign Regiment (the storied Foreign Legion) remaining through 1870.

Throughout 1863–64 and into 1865, French and Imperial troops expanded their hold on Mexico, occupying the cities of Guadalajara, Acapulco, Durango, and Oaxaca, and gaining control in other regions from the Rio Grande to the Central Valley. The Juárez government, pressed to the limit, retreated from one place to another until it reached El Paso del Norte (present Ciudad Juárez) on the Rio Grande. Republican generals, understanding their inability to confront the invaders in conventional warfare, withdrew their armies to the northern and southern frontiers, fighting a guerrilla war, building their strength, and waiting for the tide to turn.

The tide began to turn in 1865, when the U.S. Civil War came to an end. Despite professions of support for Juárez and the refusal to recognize Maximilian, the United States could do little more than lodge diplomatic protests so long as it prosecuted its own war. But this changed in early 1865 as it became clear that the final defeat of the Southern Confederacy was at hand. While Secretary of State William Seward pursued a diplomatic settlement to get French troops out of Mexico, General Grant and others prepared to use force if necessary. And Grant had plenty of force at his disposal.[6]

In May and June, 1865, while Brevet Brigadier General Salm and his men moved to Dalton and then to Atlanta, Federal authorities addressed the situation south of the border. With some 900,000 mostly battle-tested soldiers still in uniform, the Armies of the United States ranked among the world's most formidable fighting forces. In late May, as Washington prepared for a grand review of the victorious armies of Meade and Sherman, Grant ordered Major General Philip Sheridan, one of the men most responsible for his success, to take control of events west of the Mississippi. But Sheridan's main objective became to present a show of force on the Rio Grande—unofficial intimidation on a large scale. To accomplish this, Sheridan would have in Texas three corps of infantry and two large cavalry divisions, some 50,000 troops in all, un-der such proven campaigners as Major Generals Wesley Merritt and George Armstrong Custer. Despite U.S. claims of neutrality in the Mexican conflict, and with Federal officials from Grant on down look-ing the other way, thousands of rifles, surplus uniforms, tons of ammu-nition, and even some artillery pieces managed to make it into the hands of Mexico's Republican soldiers. Although plans for large formations of U.S. volunteers commanded by "volunteer" generals never got off the drawing board, an estimated 3,000 Federal veterans joined the Repub-lican ranks south of the border. The United States might not intervene directly, but it would make sure that Juárez had the means to expel the Europeans. This much Salm should have known.[7]

The Salm-Salms might also have known that by October things had begun to change in Mexico. The Republicans were making some progress in recapturing territory; the French had started to withdraw isolated garrisons. And guerrilla activity had reached problematic levels, enough that kind-hearted Maximilian regrettably bent to the machinations of his more radical advisors. On October 3, 1865, Maximilian issued the so-called "Black Decree," which mandated the summary execution of Mexicans found in unauthorized possession of arms. By this decree, dozens of Mexicans of known or suspected Republican sympathies went before Imperial firing squads. This dashed any support the empire en-joyed outside of monarchical Europe and insured Maximilian's own bloody demise.

As Agnes and Felix lobbied in Washington and New York in Febru-ary of 1866, preparing for his departure to Mexico, they must have heard of the Black Decree and known that the United States had demanded the withdrawal of French troops from Mexico. They surely knew that Salm stood virtually alone among Federal veterans in his desire to serve Maximilian. They might also have known that the expected influx of former Confederates to Maximilian's cause had not amounted to much. Yet they went ahead with their plans. Salm, therefore, sailed from victory to almost certain defeat. But such was the lot of the knight-errant.[8]

In Mexico, Salm did not receive the welcome he had expected. He found his efforts to acquire a position blocked by the intrigues of the Austrian minister, who, according to Salm, opposed any Prussian officer. The minister had some legitimate reasons; Prussia and Austria were on the verge of war—a brief, bloody, seven-week war that culminated in the decisive Prussian victory at Sadowa on July 3. But in Mexico, European rivals found themselves allies. Baron Anton von Magnus, Prussian minister to Mexico, intervened and secured for Salm an audience with Maximilian, who proved receptive. He informed Salm that rumors circulating in the capital pegged him as an impostor, prompting the cold reception he had experienced. Thanks to Magnus, Salm on July 1, 1866, received an appointment as colonel on the staff of the French commander of the Mexico City garrison. No sooner had he found employment than he requested leave so that he might bring his princess to Mexico. At Veracruz he met with the most dangerous enemy of Europeans in Mexico—the dreaded yellow fever—to which, he admitted, "I nearly became a victim." Somehow he recovered, and quickly. But, alarmed that Agnes had not arrived, he sailed for New York.[9]

The prince and princess met quite accidentally at Havana. She had sailed late from New York and had not reached Cuba until August 13, and then her ship and all its passengers went into forced quarantine. Salm noticed the protest signed by Agnes and other passengers and found his wife. Together they sailed for Mexico, arriving at Veracruz on August 24.[10]

Agnes found her introduction to Mexico inauspicious, indeed frightening. On entering Veracruz, she wrote, "you feel a shuddering creep over your whole body, for you are entering an atmosphere reminding you of the catacombs, coming from the surrounding swamps from which a tropical sun distills poisons." True enough; thousands of Europeans and Americans, would-be invaders, never made it out of Veracruz. After one night there they moved inland, but this presented more problems—bandits plagued the road to Mexico City. Worse still, a surly driver refused to allow Jimmy the dog aboard the coach, but, Agnes recalled, "the almighty dollar softened his heart." The trip brought a flurry of new experiences—tortillas and *pulque,* a fermented beverage drawn from the ubiquitous maguey plant—and a mixture of exotic scenery. Despite her initial disappointment on the coast, she found the colonial cities of Orizaba and Puebla and their surrounding mountains much more pleasing. They proceeded to Mexico City without incident and arrived on the fourth anniversary of their wedding, August 30, 1866.[11]

Salm maintained that after their arrival in Mexico City "one of the ministers" proposed that the couple return to Washington and use their influence with the president and members of Congress to secure U.S. recognition of the empire. They would have $2 million in gold to augment their influence. According to Agnes, Baron von Magnus approached her with the idea, "As I was well acquainted not only with President Johnson and most of the influential persons in the United States, but also with the best ways and means in which to work upon them." It was her show: "The proposition pleased me very much, for success seemed by no means improbable, and the importance of the mission and the confidence placed in me flattered my ambition. I therefore placed myself at the disposition of the Emperor, but Salm opposed my going alone to the United States, and insisted on going with me. He had very little diplomatic talent, and did not understand how to deal with Americans as I did. I knew that he would rather render my task more difficult, but as he obstinately insisted I could not refuse him." Of course, neither Agnes nor Felix, nor anyone else for that matter, had that kind of influence in Washington. But before this ridiculous idea took shape the empire began to crumble. Indeed, it was already well on the way to collapse.[12]

In the spring of 1866 France pulled the plug on its Mexican adventure. Under orders from Marshal Achille Bazaine, the French troops upon which Maximilian depended for survival had been withdrawing from frontier garrisons for months. But in late May, Emperor Napoleon III, under pressure from the United States and wary of Prussia's intentions on the Rhine, officially abandoned Maximilian. He announced that all French soldiers would be out of Mexico by the fall of 1867, and the withdrawal would begin at once. This, of course, violated the Treaty of Miramar and deprived Maximilian of his main source of support, support he needed until his empire coalesced, which he still believed could happen. But Napoleon's betrayal removed those beliefs. The French emperor hoped that Maximilian would abdicate, in which case his soldiers should help establish a new Mexican government (to protect French interests) before they left. Maximilian's first impulse had been to abdicate, but the ambitious Carlota, the more strong willed of the two, appealed to his honor and his pride. He decided to stay, for now, and Carlota would go to Europe and force Napoleon to change his mind. Already showing signs of paranoia, she failed to convert the troubled French emperor. Undaunted, she went to Rome to plead her case to Pope Pius IX. Here Maximilian's stubborn refusal to restore Church primacy in Mexico came into play. The Pope, while sympathetic, refused to help. At that Carlota's mind gave way. Rushed into seclusion on the orders of her brother, King Leopold II of Belgium, she would never return to Mexico or ever see her husband again. Word of Carlota's decline reached Maximilian in October. By that time he had already yielded to conservative pressures, removing all liberal voices from his government. Now prostrated by despair, he weighed his few remaining options.

The Salm-Salms reviewed their options as well, but they appeared resolved to stay in Mexico. "An idle life was utterly disgusting to me," wrote Felix, "and I heartily desired to see active service in the field." Agnes added, "The life we were leading was pleasant enough, but my Hotspur Felix panted for war. Though as kind-hearted as could be, and gentle as a lamb, he had the pugnacious instincts of a fighting-cock. War was his very element." He applied for and received permission to join Maximilian's Belgian contingent as a volunteer. In November he took the field with a Belgian battalion, and Agnes and Jimmy went along.[13]

The first day out, the column, under the haughty and disagreeable Colonel Alfred Van der Smissen, suspected an attack and prepared to fight. As Agnes recalled: "I wouldn't be left behind. I declared I would rather brave the dangers of battle than those awaiting me, perhaps, if I was left behind. Van der Smissen smiled, advised me not to fire my revolver at a distance, but to save my six shots for a hand-to-hand fight. Salm made an angry face and dropped his lorgnette [field glass], but I joyously pressed my horse between both of theirs at the head of the troops, and we advanced at a quick pace." The supposed enemy turned out to be an Austrian detachment. "I spurred my horse, and when I reached them and told them that we did not want to kill them at all, they were extremely glad, and I do not wonder that some very frightened Catholics mistook me for the Holy Virgin or some angel on horseback, dispatched expressly by their patron saint to save them." Agnes failed to mention what she did with Jimmy, who usually rode on her saddle, during her charge, and Salm made no mention of the incident at all. With the emergency passed, the column moved on.[14]

At Tulancingo (Hidalgo), about 150 kilometers northeast of Mexico City, the Belgians and attached Imperial Mexican troops were besieged by Republican forces. According to Salm, his experience included, in addition to readying a defensive perimeter, a gallant parlay over cigars and brandy with a Republican colonel. In late December, Van der Smissen received orders from Marshal Bazaine to surrender the town to the Republicans and retreat under a flag of truce toward Mexico City. The men already knew that the Belgian contingent had been disbanded earlier in the month; they would be going home. The Salm-Salms should have followed suit, but that would never do. At Buena Vista, on the road between Mexico City and Puebla, the command halted to await further instructions, and there Salm began his search for another position.[15]

Buena Vista was a popular stop between the capital and Veracruz. A nineteen-year-old Paris-born American, Sara Yorke, leaving Mexico after five years there with her parents, happened by the Belgian encampment. She recalled that "we saw at some distance, against a background formed by the Belgian camp, Princess Salm-Salm, in her gray-and-silver uniform, sitting her horse like a female centaur—a truly picturesque figure, with her white *couvre-nugue* [a forage cap with a white cover and sun-curtain] glistening under the tropical sun." Miss Yorke proved more generous than most women in her appraisal of Agnes, noting that the princess "shared the fatigues and dangers of camp life in war time—like a *Soldadera*, contemptuously said her proud sisters in society; for this mode of existence naturally drew upon her the criticism of the more conventional of her sex in the Mexican colony."[16]

At Buena Vista, the Salm-Salms learned that the emperor would pass through on his way from Orizaba to Mexico City. Maximilian had gone to Orizaba with every intention of proceeding to Veracruz—and Europe. In fact, most everyone expected the final announcement any day. The anguish he experienced over Carlota's madness left him open to the proddings of Bazaine on one hand and honest friends who hoped to spare his life on the other. Without her he had no desire to stay in Mexico. Besides, the military situation had only gotten worse. The French accelerated their departure. In November Oaxaca fell to the Republicans, followed soon by Guanajuato and San Luis Potosí, leaving only Mexico City, Puebla, Veracruz, and Querétaro as places of importance still in Imperialist possession. The empire now controlled only a tiny fraction of Mexico. And the Republicans, many wearing U.S. uniforms and accoutrements and carrying U.S. surplus rifles, gathered like a storm on the constricted empire's fringes. The new year brought nothing but dire prospects.

But at Orizaba Maximilian convened a council of conservative leaders to debate his abdication; he would abide by their decision. The conservatives still hoped to retain control and needed Maximilian to stay on, at least for a while. They voted against abdication and at the same time promised to raise money to continue the war. Division General Miguel Miramón, a former conservative president while still in his twenties, promised to bulk up the army and lead it against the Republicans. With these inducements, and under the considerable influence of the shady Jesuit Father Augustin Fischer, Maximilian vowed to remain on the throne until he could convene a special congress to determine his future. Significantly, he took the opportunity to repeal the Black Decree, perhaps as a last stab of defiance toward the conservatives, into whose hands he had placed his fate. On a more personal level, he saw little choice but to stay. His mother and his brother, the Austrian emperor, wrote to him, appealing to his honor and that of the Hapsburgs to do his duty. And then he really had no place to go; when he accepted the Mexican crown his brother stripped him of all hereditary rights. So he would return to the capital and face his destiny with a grim courage that stirred even the admiration of his enemies.[17]

It was under these circumstances that Agnes and Felix met the emperor's party at Buena Vista, but the somber procession moved on to Ayotla. Salm followed and, through Father Fischer, gained an audience with Maximilian. He requested and received permission to raise a cavalry regiment from the various departing foreign contingents. Part of the fallout from Maximilian's decision to stay became that an angry Napoleon demanded the withdrawal of all French troops as soon as practicable. The Belgian and Austrian contingents had already been disbanded and were awaiting transport to Europe. Some of the Europeans chose to stay in Mexico; from these Salm hoped to raise his regiment, but the Austrians, some 1,000 in all, merged into the Imperial Mexican Army as distinct units, leaving Salm few potential recruits. He and Agnes moved on to Mexico City unemployed. Again through Father Fischer, a fellow German, he asked for a position, but nothing came up.[18]

In the capital on February 5, 1867, Felix and Agnes watched from their hotel balcony the departure of the last French troops, the hated Marshal Bazaine and his pretty young Mexican wife in the lead. The French soldiers shouted their intentions now to march on Berlin—a reference to the growing tensions between France and Prussia. "I did not regard their talk," wrote Salm, "but I only wished to be in Berlin to meet them there." Despite the uncertainty caused by the French departure, and the vulnerable state in which it left the empire, most people in the capital were glad to see them go. Now, for the most part, the situation more resembled the civil war that it really always had been.[19]

As the foreign troops marched away from Mexico City, Imperialist forces began to concentrate at the colonial city of Querétaro. The Republicans, meanwhile, closed in for the kill. Maximilian's General Miramón, with the emperor's blessing, launched an effort to upset the Juarista momentum—the capture of Juárez or another leading Republican. Miramón led a picked column of 4,000 men to the city of Zacatecas, some 400 kilometers northwest of Mexico City, where Juárez, following his armies, had established his headquarters. Miramón took Zacatecas by surprise, but Juárez and his ministers managed to escape. Juarista Division General Mariano Escobedo soon cornered Miramón's outnumbered command and routed it, capturing the Imperial war chest, several pieces of artillery, and about 1,500 prisoners, of whom some 100 were shot, including Miramón's brother. Most of those executed were former French Legionnaires, who had stayed behind and joined the Imperial army. Since foreign troops had been ordered out of Mexico and granted safe passage, Juárez considered those remaining filibusters, subject to the death penalty. Word of this should have added a final inducement for Salm to get out while he could, but, apparently, the thought never crossed his mind.

Marshal Bazaine, en route to Veracruz, learned of the Miramón disaster and again offered Maximilian a way out. The emperor, thoroughly disgusted with the French, did not even respond. Bazaine bore the brunt of resentment in Mexico, but for the most part he only followed Napoleon's directives, and the deals he made with the Juaristas for the evacuation of the French and other foreign contingents likely saved thousands of lives. They also seriously compromised the Mexican empire. In Europe, Napoleon had already cast Bazaine as the scapegoat for his own ill-advised Mexican adventure. Once the French sailed away, Maximilian was doomed.[20]

With the empire constricted now to a handful of major points—Mexico City, Veracruz, Puebla, and Querétaro—and with most of the foreign troops gone, the Salm-Salms' decision to stay appeared reckless at best. Just what considerations made them stay neither Agnes nor Felix articulated, other than to satisfy Salm's lust for battle and Agnes's strange obsession with courting influence. But little glory appeared in the offing, and Maximilian had no influence to dispense. At this point, Salm had not had the opportunity to develop the kind of personal relationship with Maximilian that his actions indicated, and Agnes had yet even to meet the emperor. Salm may have possessed the kind of sanguinary recklessness that passed for gallantry in the nineteenth century. As Agnes wrote of her husband's martial enthusiasm, "That he once, when still a boy, was left with seven wounds on the battle-field, did not cure him. . . . A shot in his right arm, which was rather dangerous, received in a duel, did not cure him either. . . . He was like a cocked pistol, every moment ready to go off." Clearly, Salm believed he could satisfy his blood lust in Mexico. But that did not explain Agnes's motivation; she had little to gain as things stood. Despite her boasting, she now needed Salm more than he needed her.[21]

As Imperial Mexico braced for a final stand, Salm had no place in the plans. Back at the capital, Mexican conservatives went to work on Maximilian, isolating him from the few remaining European influences who might yet persuade him to abdicate. As long as Maximilian held the throne, and the Imperial army, such as it was, held together, conservative leaders believed that some compromise with Juárez might still be reached. With him gone the army would crumble into factions, and the conservatives would have no chips with which to bargain—nothing would stop the Juaristas from storming the capital and exacting a bloody toll. It was a slim hope, but then the conservatives had few options.

At some point after the French withdrawal, Maximilian resolved to take the field as supreme commander of the Imperial Mexican Army.

Division General Leonardo Márquez, infamous for his slaughter of civilians following a conservative victory at Tacubaya in 1859, convinced Maximilian that the time had come for him to cut himself free of foreign soldiers. Mexico would provide his soldiers. So as he prepared to march out of the capital and take command of the Imperial forces gathering at Querétaro, word went out that the two Austrian regiments would not be going, no foreign soldiers would be going. It was complete fiction. The Imperial army contained hundreds of foreign soldiers—soldiers of fortune, former Legionnaires, men from a dozen nationalities—but the emperor's prized Austrians were ordered to remain in Mexico City. This accomplished two important goals for the conservatives: Maximilian's role as supreme commander would limit the rivalries among Mexican generals, and separating him from his loyal Austrians removed him from their influence.

When Felix Salm-Salm learned that Maximilian planned to take the field, he rushed to Baron Magnus, asking the Prussian minister to secure permission for him to accompany the emperor. He learned that no foreigners would be permitted to go. When on February 13 he heard the sounds of marching soldiers in the streets, he could not believe the twist of fate that kept him from the fighting. "It seemed to me against nature that I should not accompany the Emperor on his expedition," Salm wrote, "and I was very unhappy." He hastened to Baron Magnus, "hoping to find some consolation." According to Agnes, Magnus "found some other means to satisfy the pugnacious longings of my impetuous Felix." The minister suggested that Salm approach Division General Santiago Vidaurri, then preparing to lead a secondary column to join Maximilian, about taking him along. Vidaurri, who once controlled the states of Nuevo León, Coahuila, and Tamaulipas as a liberal before he fell out with Juárez, agreed to take Salm if the secretary of war approved. With the help of Magnus, Salm got the necessary documents and prepared to go.[22]

This time the Soldier Princess would not be going along, and she did not take the news well. "I of course expected to go with Salm as usual, but for once he refused in a most determined manner and remained deaf to all my entreaties. Now it was my turn to become mad. I cried and screamed so as to be heard two blocks off; and Jimmy, who felt for his mistress, howled and barked; but Salm stole away and took a street where he could not hear me and I not see him. I believe I hated him at that moment, and felt very unhappy, for I knew he would come to grief, having never any luck without me." Her outburst did her no good. She would stay in the comfortable residence of friends. Salm at last had his wish, he marched out of Mexico City with Vidaurri's column, following Maximilian to Querétaro.[23]

CHAPTER 5

"Well, Colonel, Here Am I"

For the time being Agnes waited. She might believe in her ability to affect events, but this one remained far beyond her powers. She had no passion for Mexico and no respect for its people. And now, removed from the main stage, she missed the opportunity to shine. In her despair over Salm's solitary departure, and with her grudging recognition that he probably was correct in leaving her behind, not even the Soldier Princess could have imagined the turn of events that would bring her back to center stage.

Salm had joined a death march, plain and simple, and he did so willingly. With Vidaurri, he left Mexico City only hours after the emperor, escorted by a detachment of Austrian hussars who, like Salm, took this opportunity to join the emperor, and Don Santiago's personal bodyguard of *caballeros* from northern Mexico, some forty soldiers in all. Vidaurri's presence with the army, Maximilian hoped, would attract support from his traditional stronghold in the northeast as the Imperialists moved in that direction. His more immediate role was to bring the funds that

Maximilian's ministers had promised for the campaign. They had promised millions; they delivered only "50,000 miserable pesos."[1]

This posed the latest in a series of disappointments that confronted Maximilian when he began his march to Querétaro. General Márquez had led the emperor to believe that he would have 10,000 men for the march, but when Maximilian met his command on the morning of February 13, he found only 1,600 soldiers ready to march. It was a bad omen.

Late at night on the first day's march Vidaurri's detachment caught up with the main column at Cuautitlán. Salm shared a cold camp with other officers in the yard of a hacienda. The next morning Maximilian reviewed his troops, not in the dress of a European monarch but in that of a Mexican general. Salm described the scene: "The Emperor was received by the troops with great enthusiasm. He mounted a very fine piebald horse, with Mexican saddle and bridle, wore the general's coat without epaulets, dark trousers, and over them boots reaching up to his knees, and a large Mexican sombrero. He was armed with a sabre, and two revolvers attached to the saddle. He held always in his hand a single, very simple field-glass, through which he scanned the country before him very frequently." As Maximilian rode along the line he came to Vidaurri and Salm, and on seeing the prince he initiated an exchange:

> "Zounds! Salm, how did you come here?"
>
> "Your Majesty would not take me with you, . . . and as I would not remain idle in Mexico, I requested General Vidaurri to take me with him."
>
> "You know the reasons why I refused your request; however, I am very glad to see you here."

The march continued. The next two days passed without incident, but on the third the column came under attack at San Miguel Calpulálpan. Maximilian displayed cool courage in the fight, in which his troops prevailed. To pleas from General Vidaurri and Dr. Samuel Basch to take cover, the emperor replied, "I am of no use if I spare myself at the first opportunity." At one point Salm pursued and attempted to capture a Juarista cavalryman, but the soldier raised his carbine and, according to Salm, "I had just the time to fire, and sent a bullet through his head." Trailing Imperial troops perforated the corpse with lances, "according to the bad Mexican fashion." Maximilian lost only one man in the brief battle, but his Hungarian cook took a spent ball in the mouth, which Salm recalled, left "his tasting faculties . . . spoiled for some time."[2]

Maximilian and his little army arrived at Querétaro on February 19 to a grand welcome. The colonial city of some 40,000 inhabitants had long been a conservative stronghold. Here the various Imperial field armies converged in preparation for a move against the Republicans. Maximilian and his generals hoped to defeat three threatening Juarista armies in detail before they too could concentrate. It was Maximilian's only chance; if the Republicans came together they would outnumber significantly the Imperial army. The Republican forces also possessed a considerable advantage in small arms, including repeating rifles from the United States, and artillery. They had the intangible benefits of momentum and morale as well. So even as Maximilian enjoyed the lavish welcome staged for his benefit, military reality conspired against him.

The inadequacy of Maximilian's command, despite all the promises, became apparent at once. General Miramón had arrived from his disastrous raid in Zacatecas with what remained of his force, which, combined with the men that Márquez brought from the capital, amounted to about 3,000 in all arms. The talented Indian Division General Tomás Mejía came in with another 2,000, after they had skillfully fought their way south from Matamoros on the Rio Grande. On February 22 Brigade General Ramón Méndez arrived with his crack command from Michoacán, bringing another 4,000 men. With only 9,000 soldiers and thirty-five guns, the Imperial army hardly packed the punch necessary for offensive operations. In fact, it would be hard-pressed to stand on defense. Maximilian sent for the remaining foreign troops and field artillery in Mexico City, but the ministers, fearing for their own well-being, would not release them. Maximilian had all the men, give or take a few, that he could expect.

Salm, without an official position, passed his time as well as he could, going to the theater and to a bull fight that he described as "half-disgusting half-laughable." But in early March, Republican troops began to appear. The emperor, who established himself in a forward position on *El Cerro de las Campanas* (the Hill of the Bells), offered Salm the command of an elite battalion of *Cazadores* (light infantry), which the prince quickly accepted. As further evidence of the fiction of an all-Mexican army, Salm's battalion of 700 contained only 150 Mexicans; the rest being mostly French, with some Germans and Hungarians as well. "It was a wild corps," Salm reported, "of the bravest soldiers that could be found." The prince and his Cazadores took their place in line.[3]

The Imperial troops, while small in number, represented some of the best soldiers in Mexico, and soon they found opportunity to prove it. On March 14 the Republican forces of General Mariano Escobedo attacked Querétaro. In this first major battle of the campaign the emperor again displayed bold leadership, exposing himself to constant enemy fire. And Salm finally got satisfactory exposure. "Colonel Prince Salm-Salm," Dr. Basch wrote, "made a brilliant sortie and captured a cannon." Salm claimed that his Cazadores killed 300 men and took dozens of prisoners in addition to a fine Parrot rifled gun. It was a clear victory for the Imperial army, but one that would be difficult to repeat. Querétaro, surrounded as it was by hills, offered a most accommodating target for the rapidly encroaching Juaristas.[4]

Maximilian began to seek Salm's advice on military matters. After the victory of the fourteenth, Salm advocated a vigorous offensive drive to San Luis Potosí. His general contempt for Mexican soldiers led him to believe that Escobedo's soldiers would be so discouraged over their defeat that it would take days for them to rally. He misjudged Escobedo, and he misjudged the new spirit of the Republican army. Maximilian, however, yielded to his chief of staff, Márquez, who insisted on a stand at Querétaro. Salm's idea may have been unrealistic, but the decision to stand a siege amounted to a death sentence for the empire. By this time, though, it did not matter much; the Republicans had Querétaro pretty well surrounded with four times Maximilian's number.[5]

Still, Salm's star was on the rise. On March 20 Maximilian gave him command of a brigade in General Méndez's Reserve Division. On Salm's recommendation the Cazadores went to Austrian Major Ernst Pitner, who recently had been released by Escobedo on his promise to leave Mexico. He, like Salm, could not resist a fight. On March 22 Salm played a conspicuous role in a raid on nearby San Juanico to capture reported Republican artillery and food stores. Although the raid netted some twenty wagons of corn and small arms and some livestock, the artillery had been removed.[6]

If the situation at Querétaro held out little hope, the greater predicament was even worse. By March 20, Maximilian came to understand that the ministry in Mexico City had forsaken him. The reinforcements he ordered had not arrived, nor had the funds he was promised. He resolved to send Generals Márquez and Vidaurri to Mexico City to oust the culprits and rush aid to the beleaguered garrison. Márquez was to assume control of the capital while Vidaurri took direction of the ministry. The bloodthirsty Márquez had been chiefly responsible for the situation; he more than anyone else had convinced Maximilian to stay; he had convinced him to leave the foreign troops in the capital; he had advocated that Maximilian hold at Querétaro; and now he took the first opportunity to quit the sinking ship. At this point, the emperor retained faith in his general, but his confidence was misplaced. After midnight on the twenty-third, Márquez, Vidaurri, and 1,200 cavalry rode through the Republican lines and made for the capital, promising to return in a fortnight.[7]

Perceiving an opportunity after the departure of 1,200 soldiers, the Republicans attacked in force the next day. Salm again performed well in repulsing the Juaristas, and his connection with the emperor grew. He recalled a particularly poignant scene:

> The enthusiasm of the troops was tremendous when the Emperor appeared on the battle-ground. He rode up to me and pressed my hand. He had tears in his eyes, and was so deeply agitated that he could not speak; but he whispered three words which made me happier than any decoration whatever could have done—words that will re-echo in my memory and heart until the end of my life. I also was so affected that I could not utter single word, but silently kissed that generous hand which rested in mine. Only he who has experienced such moments can understand the feelings produced by them; they are not to be described. (Salm did not identify the three words.)

The bond between Maximilian and Salm, born of mutual admiration, would continue to grow. The *New York Herald* reported, "The most intimate friend and counsellor of the Emperor is now Prince Salm-Salm, who since the departure of Marquez, has virtually been his Chief of Staff." But the brave defenders of Querétaro could withstand only a few more attacks before numbers began to tell, and Republican guns on the surrounding hills reminded the Imperialists who held the upper hand.[8]

Fourteen days passed without word from Márquez, and while the emperor retained at least a show of faith in the general, the other defenders had their doubts. They continued to fight valiantly, with Salm's command always carrying a heavy load—he believed that Miramón kept putting him in harm's way in order to get rid of him. But the men, including Maximilian, were down to eating horse and mule. And dissension among the officers, always a concern, came to the surface. Méndez hated Miramón, who maintained the viability of standing firm. Mejía and Méndez, both brave and loyal soldiers, now advocated a breakout. Still, the emperor held out for Márquez.[9]

Back in Mexico City, an anxious Agnes found herself in a much better position to know what General Márquez was up to, but that did her husband little good. "For many weeks we heard nothing from Queretaro but vague reports, and of a very contradictory unreliable kind" she recalled. She at once went to see Márquez, who received her "very graciously," and told her of Salm's bravery. Then she saw Vidaurri. He repeated the stories of her husband's feats in battle and informed her that "all was going extremely well" at Querétaro. But after a few days of festivities, during which nothing was done for the relief of Maximilian, Márquez resolved to attack the Republican forces of Porfirio Díaz, the talented young division general who now threatened Puebla. Márquez led an army that included the Austrian brigade, which should have been on its way to Querétaro, and had not reached Puebla before he learned that the important city had already fallen. The Imperial troops tried to return to Mexico City, but the aggressive Díaz caught up. Márquez's command shattered on impact, the general being among the first to take flight. Only the Austrians maintained any order; they delayed the inspired Republican pursuit, but not by much. "Marquez," Agnes reported, "accompanied only by twelve horsemen, returned a fugitive, twelve hours in advance of his whole army." By April 12, Agnes could watch as the Republicans moved into the suburbs of Mexico City, beginning a siege of the capital. "During the following night," she recalled, "I dreamt that I saw my husband dying." After two more nights of such dreams, Agnes resolved to "try what I could do to save the Emperor and my husband."[10]

Over the next several days Agnes passed back and forth between the lines, trying to arrange a deal for the surrender of Mexico City in exchange for the safe passage of Maximilian and the other foreigners from the country, although she had no such authority. According to her, she was fired upon by both sides during her efforts. The thirty-six-year-old General Díaz, who commanded the Republican Army of the South,

agreed to see Agnes and appeared amiable enough under the circumstances. He would not discuss the surrender of the capital—he could
take it in due time and intended to execute enemies of the republic such
as the murderer Márquez—but if the foreign troops chose to surrender
he would guarantee their passage to any port. As for Maximilian and
Querétaro, he had no authority, although he would provide Agnes with
a pass to see General Escobedo. On April 27 Agnes, with a civilian
escort, two unarmed coachmen, her maid, and Jimmy the terrier left
Mexico City in a bright yellow carriage bound for Querétaro.[11]

Agnes could not have known that in the time since Márquez left,
the situation in Querétaro had deteriorated dramatically. On April 15
Maximilian had resolved to send another detachment after Márquez,
this time under the capable Mejía. But the brave Indian was ill; so on
Maximilian's insistence Salm would lead the mission. The Prince received extensive instructions from the emperor, ranging from directions to the diplomatic corps to authorization to arrest Márquez if
reports of his treason proved accurate. In the early morning darkness
of the eighteenth, Salm and a picked escort led by some Mexican cavalry
failed to break the enemy line and had to abandon the mission. Salm,
who received a slight leg wound in the action, blamed the failure on
the Mexican officer charged with the breakout and hinted at treachery—
he believed that the Republicans had been alerted. Treachery or not,
the conditions now made any breakout next to impossible. The Imperial
force had dwindled to some 6,500, while the Republican host continued to gather strength; Escobedo's army now outnumbered the defenders by about 35,000 men.[12]

On April 21 Maximilian appointed Salm first aide-de-camp and, later
that week, chief of the emperor's household, but these served as the only
bright moments in an otherwise bleak existence. The next day,
Maximilian learned that Puebla had fallen and that Márquez had been
routed. Now all thoughts turned to a breakout. Several plans had been
discussed, including a limited escape by Maximilian and a picked escort,
but Maximilian refused to abandon the army that had stood by him. On
April 27, the same day that Agnes started for Querétaro, the Imperial
army attempted to break out. After great initial success, General Miramón
decided to turn the breakout into a general battle, and the Republicans
rallied, driving the Imperial troops back into the city. Salm implored the
emperor to follow the original plan to leave, but Miramón won him over

with plans to enlarge the attack the following day. Maximilian thus lost his last realistic chance to escape. Over the next week Imperial troops made several largely unsuccessful sorties against the ever-tightening Republican envelopment, all to no avail.[13]

During the first week of May, Agnes arrived at Querétaro in her yellow carriage, looking for General Escobedo. She rode to Escobedo's headquarters, where she encountered a young captain who addressed her "as an old acquaintance from the United States, though," she noted, "I did not remember his face." It turned out that he had served in the German Division and had once escorted her during a trip to General Blenker's camp. This captain, she later learned, "boasted that 'he knew me intimately.'" Such was her reputation.

General Escobedo, a most capable soldier and a veteran of the War of the Reform, commanded the Republican Army of the North, but at Querétaro he assumed command of all forces in the vicinity. According to Agnes, "He received me very kindly, and I told him I heard that my husband was wounded, and requested his permission to go into the city." The general said he could not grant her such permission, but he would give her a letter of introduction to President Juárez at San Luis Potosí, who alone could give her such permission. Escobedo admitted that he knew of her husband as "an extremely brave officer, as he had experienced to his great damage." Still, the general promised to treat Salm well should he be captured and provided Agnes with the necessary letters for Juárez. With that, she headed to San Luis Potosí.[14]

She arrived at the temporary capital of the republic after a journey of three days. Once settled in a fine residence, she called on President Juárez, incredibly, with her dog Jimmy. "The President gave me his hand," she wrote, "led me to the sofa, on which Jimmy had already established himself, and said he would listen to what I had to say." That she would take her dog on this visit represented the kind of unprincipled behavior that attracted negative comments. That she would allow that dog to make himself at home in the president's office reflected remarkably poor manners at best, but it more likely evidenced a completely self-centered ignorance of decorum. (She would later be horrified when Jimmy took station on Maximilian's bed.) Kind Juárez no doubt had more important issues to contemplate, but he listened courteously before informing Agnes that he had no details from Querétaro and could not grant her request to enter that city until he heard from General Escobedo. He did suggest that she remain in San Luis Potosí, as Querétaro should fall within days. It was good advice.[15]

Cinco de Mayo dawned quietly; it was the fifth anniversary of the 1862 Mexican victory over the French at Puebla. For much of the day the defenders of Querétaro listened as Republican troops celebrated with drink and cheers. But that evening the Juaristas opened with the largest artillery barrage of the siege, followed by an all-out infantry assault, resulting only in piles of dead attackers, felled by timely blasts of canister. The Imperialists had withstood numerous attacks, but morale dwindled anyway and desertions escalated dramatically; food was scarce, and everyone from Maximilian on down knew that no help was coming. Always the optimist, Salm noted in typical Salm fashion, "We still had wine." The generals continued to toy with ideas of escape. During these dark days, Maximilian walked about the trenches with Salm, constantly drawing fire. "Shells and balls struck near us in disagreeable quantities," Prince Felix wrote, "but none of them would satisfy the secret longing of the Emperor."[16]

A *New York Herald* correspondent reported from Querétaro that Maximilian indeed appeared deliberately to court death: "Once when he stood in the plaza for ten minutes, while the shells were bursting so near him that the concussion of the air nearly carried him off his balance, this idea was regarded as a fixed fact." The correspondent continued: "'My firm belief,' said Prince Salm-Salm afterward, in his quaint broken English, `is dhat he vaunted to be killed; only I vish ven he vants to do dat again he vill take somebody else mit him, not me.'" While Salm made frequent mentions of this kind of activity, he always claimed that he stood prepared to share his emperor's fate.[17]

During a council of war on May 11 the generals determined to break out at all costs. Over the next three days, preparations went ahead. Salm maintained that Maximilian took this opportunity to promote him to general but requested that he keep it to himself until after the evacuation for fear of jealousy among the Mexican generals. The breakout, scheduled for May 14, was pushed back to the next day. As it turned out it was a day too late. That night Colonel Miguel López, a particular favorite of the emperor, sold out to General Escobedo. He would lead Republican troops into the city, but, apparently, Maximilian was to be allowed to escape. Everything went as planned: Republican soldiers moved into the city, and surprised Imperial soldiers surrendered *en masse*—but Maximilian refused to play along. Alerted by the traitor López, Salm rushed to the emperor, who too had been warned. Maximilian, with Salm, Mejía, and several others, moved to El Cerro da las Campanas and there tried to rally the army. Miramón was shot in the face and captured; Méndez managed to hide. On the Hill of Bells, Maximilian said to Salm, "now for a lucky bullet." His wish again went unanswered. Soon artillery and small arms fire compelled the emperor and his suite to surrender. General Méndez, who more than anyone else feared a bloody end to things, was betrayed to the Republicans and shot. The emperor, Salm, and the rest of the officers entered an uneasy captivity. The emperor's private secretary José Luis Blasio recalled a frightening moment on May 18: "At eight o'clock that night Salm-Salm was taken away." The other prisoners assumed that he would be shot, "But Salm-Salm returned in an hour, saying that the authorities merely wanted to ascertain his nationality."[18]

Agnes received the news at San Luis Potosí and immediately tried to secure a pass from Juárez, but the president was understandably unavailable. She headed to Querétaro without his blessing. She arrived on May 19, too late to see General Escobedo, but bright and early the next morning she appeared at his headquarters. Again, Escobedo received her warmly, and this time he readily complied with her wishes. He detailed Colonel Ricardo Villanueva from his staff to escort the princess to the Convent of San Teresita, where many of the prisoners were housed:

> We now entered a small dirty room, where several officers were lying about on "cocos" [horse blankets made of maguey leaves] on the floor, all looking very neglected. On asking for my husband, a polite little gentleman, M. Blasio, informed me the Prince was with the Emperor, and would return directly. He had scarcely said so when my husband came. He was not shaved, wore a collar several days old, and looked altogether as if he had emerged from a dustbin, though not worse than the rest of his comrades. To see him again under these circumstances affected me very much, and I wept and almost fainted when he held me in his arms.

Salm soon introduced his wife to Maximilian. "I shall never forget this first interview with the Emperor," she wrote. "I found him in a miserable bare room, in bed, looking very sick and pale. He received me with the utmost kindness, kissed my hand, and pressed it in his, and told me how glad he was that I had come." She informed the fallen emperor of events in Mexico City and of her talk with President Juárez, and that the prevailing opinion held that Maximilian and his officers would be shot.[19]

Agnes suggested that she return to Escobedo and enter into negotiations in the name of the emperor, which she did with his blessings. She found the victorious general "in a very good humor." He said that he could not go to Maximilian, but that he would receive him and the Salm-Salms that afternoon. When the time came, Maximilian took Agnes's arm and, escorted by Colonel Villanueva and a small guard, they traveled to Escobedo's headquarters outside of the city. Escobedo welcomed them in his usual cordial manner, and after some polite conversation Maximilian suggested that Salm present some propositions. Salm and Villanueva adjourned to work out the details of the proposals, as they could converse in French. Maximilian proposed through Salm to abdicate at once, never again to interfere in Mexican affairs, and to order the surrenders of Veracruz and Mexico City. In exchange, he requested that all foreign troops and such Mexican officers as so wished be transported to Veracruz and allowed to return to Europe. Escobedo promised to present these proposals to his government. According to Dr. Basch and Blasio, they feared that the emperor had been taken to be executed and were relieved when he and Salm returned that night to the convent.[20]

A *New York Herald* correspondent reported Agnes's recent efforts and also added another myth to legend: "The wife of Prince Salm-Salm, an American lady—*née* Agnes Le Clerg—closely related to President Johnson, made her way alone to San Luis Potosi to intercede with President Juarez for her husband's life as well as that of the Emperor Maximilian. This lady has sped so far in her brave mission that yesterday, on her arrival here from San Luis, herself, the Emperor and Prince Salm-Salm had a long interview with General Escobedo, and I have reason to believe that terms have been arranged by which the lives of most of the foreigners will be spared." As it turned out, the correspondent proved mostly correct, although perhaps not as he might have imagined. Much remained to be done, but Agnes had just begun to fight.[21]

"The Emperor tells me that yesterday [May 21] Princess Salm-Salm went to great lengths to secure him better quarters with a garden," recalled Dr. Basch, "specters of escape and abduction haunt her constantly." Her attempt to get better lodgings for Maximilian and her husband backfired, as it appeared that many in the Republican camp believed that the prisoners had already been treated too well. On May 22 the emperor, Salm, and the generals were removed to the Capuchin convent, where Maximilian was made to spend the night in a crypt. This was a particularly cruel punishment; for more than two hundred years Hapsburgs had been entombed in Vienna's Capuchin crypt. On visiting the emperor that night, Dr. Basch was devastated when Salm directed him to the crypt. "Calm yourself; he is alive," Salm told him, "but he really is in a crypt." Dr. Basch found his patient resting comfortably on a cot, reading by candlelight.[22]

On May 24, as Salm sat with the emperor in the yard of the convent, Colonel Miguel Palacios called Salm aside to ask him to inform Maximilian that his trial was soon to begin and he would be isolated from contact with the other prisoners. For now, only Maximilian, Mejía, and the wounded Miramón would stand trial, the details of which were only then being determined. Salm tried to get permission to visit his friend the emperor, but, he wrote ungenerously, "it is impossible to get from a Mexican a straightforward answer, and I could get nothing except some vague promises." Agnes, Salm, and Basch all included in their memoirs many such derogatory remarks, but Salm, especially, often praised his brother officers and the men who served him. He possessed particularly high regard for Méndez and Mejía. Salm, who could well have been shot on sight, received very good, even respectful, treatment, as did his wife. Their remarks, like those of Basch, reflected the general prejudice of Europeans and North Americans. But none of them seemed above seeking the good offices of the lowly Republicans.[23]

Maximilian's predicament wore heavily on Agnes, who resolved to do something about it. With Colonel Villanueva, her constant companion since her arrival at Querétaro, she developed a plan to go to President Juárez and, if nothing else, persuade him to postpone the trial until an adequate defense could be arranged. Late at night on May 25, Agnes and the colonel went to the Capuchin convent to get the emperor's approval. Past midnight, Villanueva secured their entry, and Agnes woke

Salm, who agreed with the plan and took her to Maximilian. As Agnes recalled, "Villanueva advised him to write a letter to Juárez, and request two weeks' time to prepare his defence." The Republican colonel drafted the letter, which Maximilian signed. With that, Agnes and her companion bid the emperor farewell. "I was very much affected," she wrote, "for it appeared to me as if I had now seen his face for the last time."[24]

Salm's version differed slightly. He had learned from Agnes earlier in the day that because of the Black Decree all officers in captivity would be executed. Maximilian, Miramón, and Mejía would be only the first. The rest would follow according to rank. "In this manner," Salm recalled, "I was enabled to make the interesting calculation how soon my turn would come." According to the prince, he received through Palacios admittance to the emperor, and they came up with the plan for Agnes to travel to San Luis Potosí, which they relayed to her during the late-night meeting.[25]

So while Agnes traveled again to San Luis Potosí, Salm turned his attentions to escape. After a conversation with Colonel Villanueva, in which the sympathetic officer admitted that Maximilian was as good as dead, Salm began to develop a plan of escape, systematically bribing guards and working out with the emperor an elaborate code. But Maximilian would not consider escaping without Mejía and Miramón. Salm worked accordingly, arranging for all necessities. Still, Maximilian maintained a cavalier attitude, informing Salm in a note passed hidden in a piece of bread that he needed certain supplies for a disguise, because he would not shave his beard lest he expose an embarrassingly weak chin. "On the horse," the emperor required, "two serapes, two revolvers, and a sabre. Not to forget bread or biscuit, red wine, and chocolate. A riding-whip is also necessary." Under these circumstances, Salm stood little chance of effecting an escape. But then, Maximilian may not really have wanted to escape.[26]

After leaving the convent, Agnes went to see Escobedo, amazingly, at 1 A.M. "I found him fortunately in very good humor," she recalled. He readily gave her a letter to Juárez. She then made a mad dash for San Luis Potosí, completing the trip in less than two days and with very little sleep. Juárez agreed to see her on the morning of May 28. The president initially refused her request for a delay of Maximilian's trial, at which point she claimed to have said, "Well, Mr. Juarez, . . . pray reserve your decision until at least five o'clock this afternoon. Should you remain of the same determination, then I will return to Queretaro, Heaven knows with how sad a heart." At the appointed time she returned to find that indeed Juárez had granted her request. She telegraphed the news to Querétaro and without hesitation headed there herself.[27]

Dr. Basch dejectedly recorded Agnes's return: "The news that she promised is only that a postponement has been granted." Without changing she went straight to the convent. "I was worn with fatigue; my boots torn to pieces, and my feet sore; my hair in disorder, and my face and hands unwashed; I must indeed have looked like a scarecrow," she recalled, "but I was very happy and a little proud too." Salm briefed her on the plans for escape, but, she later maintained, she had no confidence in the plan. Agnes claimed that she advanced the idea to call for Baron Magnus, the Prussian minister, and some lawyers from Mexico City, and that she would go for them. But before this could occur, the escape plan came to a head: the necessary officers were bribed; horses and supplies had been arranged. All was made ready for an escape on June 2.

On that day, though, a telegraphed message announced that Magnus and two esteemed liberal attorneys, Mariano Riva Palacio and Rafael Martínez de la Torre, were on their way to Querétaro. Maximilian would not embarrass them, and he canceled the escape. According to Agnes, "The Emperor, to whom the idea of escape had been always repugnant, was glad to find a pretext or reason to postpone it." This, of course, did not stop Agnes and Salm from trying to save the man.[28]

While Agnes was away at San Luis Potosí, Salm spent many hours with Maximilian. During one conversation, the emperor recalled that he had appointed Salm a general only verbally. "Though his powers were now at an end, he said he hoped I might require such documents, and therefore ordered Blasio to make them out." The commission was dated from May 14. The emperor also made Salm an officer of the Order of Guadalupe and created Agnes a lady of honor in the Order of San Carlos—meaningless titles as things stood, but ones that Agnes would cling to with pride for the rest of her life. The general's commission, though, could put Salm in front of a firing squad.[29]

Over the next few days, lawyers and diplomats came and went as Maximilian settled his affairs. He seemed content to accept whatever happened to him but continued to allow the Salm-Salms and others to develop escape scenarios. Salm gained permission to room with Dr. Basch near the emperor, and he spent much time in his presence. Agnes too visited frequently, never giving up her quest to see Maximilian in healthier lodgings.

Escobedo and his officers knew that escape plans had circulated for days. The general likely hoped that Maximilian would find a way out of his predicament, as he had no desire to be the executioner. Things were complicated, though, and tensions ran high. On June 5, a Republican officer informed Salm: "You have attempted to effect the escape of Maximiliano. If you repeat it you will be shot on the spot." After an angry exchange, Salm went to visit the emperor, "to take an invigorating example from the serene dignity with which he bore his cross." (Likening Maximilian's predicament to Christ's martyrdom became a common theme; the fallen emperor even had a crown of thorns nailed to the wall of his cell.) Soon an officer came for Salm, who naturally believed he was to be shot. The prince turned to Maximilian to take his leave: "When I saw him I could not utter one single word. He gave me his hand, which I covered with kisses. I felt as if I might not look on his dear face again. At the door I again looked around. Two silent tears ran down the august martyr's cheeks. That was too much. My heart was breaking. I rushed to my room, and gave vent to my grief by loud sobs." But Salm would not be executed. Like all the other officers in the convent, he was being moved away from the emperor. In order to discourage ideas of escape, Escobedo trebled the guard and deprived the prisoners of eating utensils. At this, Salm's comrades asked him to abandon all of his schemes.[30]

On June 9 and 10, the Republicans dealt summary justice to all company- and field-grade officers—prison terms of two to six years, depending on rank, at various spots throughout Mexico. By this judgment, Salm, a colonel on Republican records, received a six-year sentence at a site yet to be determined. But Salm produced his general's commission, to which a sympathetic officer informed him that he would likely be shot and offered to keep silent, but Salm refused him: "The idea of being still more separated from the Emperor, under the present circumstances, was intolerable to me." Salm, along with eleven other generals and selected field-grade officers now became subject to trial by court-martial. The trial of Maximilian, Mejía, and Miramón had already begun.[31]

Salm regained permission to see the man the Republicans called by his old-world title, Archiduque Fernando Maximiliano de Habsburgo, and Agnes had been a frequent visitor. As it became obvious to all that the trial would end with a guilty verdict and likely execution, Agnes resolved to mount one last escape attempt. Under the latest plan, Maximilian, Mejía, Miramón, and the Salm-Salms, with an escort of bought-off Juarista cavalry, would head for the fastness of the Sierra Gordo and then to Veracruz. She secured the promise of assistance from Colonel Villanueva, with whom she had been most friendly since her arrival at Querétaro. But he told her that he could do nothing without the cooperation of Colonel Palacios. Agnes's plan required bribery, but with no money available she had Maximilian sign two promissory notes for 100,000 pesos each to be honored by his brother, the emperor of Austria. Villanueva required that the checks be guaranteed by two of the foreign ministers then in the city. Maximilian gave faithful Dr. Basch the assignment of getting the required signatures, but none of the men approached would sign what amounted to a death warrant should the notes fall into the wrong hands. Still, Villanueva planned to go along. It would be up to Agnes to convert Palacios.[32]

On June 13 Agnes visited Maximilian and stayed with him until 8:00 P.M., chatting about his family and what he planned to do when he returned to Europe. He asked her, should he not make it, to assure his mother of his love. "I felt extremely sad," she recalled, "for I had a strong presentiment that I now saw him for the last time." This time she was right. On leaving the emperor, she asked Colonel Palacios to escort her home, which he agreed to do. Agnes stayed in a private residence within walking distance of the convent. She asked the nervous colonel into her parlor and engaged him in conversation. Palacios confessed that although Maximilian was his enemy, he had come to admire the manner with which he faced his misfortune. Then she cut to the point: "It was a most thrilling moment, on which indeed hung the life or death of a noble and good man, who was my friend and Emperor." After she secured his promise of confidentiality, Agnes told him that plans for the emperor's escape were in place and that all he need do was turn his back for ten minutes. For this he would receive a check from the emperor for 100,000 pesos and another 5,000 in gold (which she hoped to secure from Baron Magnus). Colonel Palacios feared for his wife and young child and declined the check with the promise to consider the offer. He would give her an answer in the morning.

Unwilling to give up, Agnes produced the emperor's signet ring, which Palacios was to give to Maximilian as a sign that the escape could proceed. The colonel refused to accept, defying the prevailing stereotype among Imperialists that any Mexican could be bribed. He cited his honor, his wife, and his child. "Well, Colonel," she said, "you are not well-disposed. Reflect about it, and remember your word of honour and your oath." Colonel Villanueva then arrived, followed by Dr. Basch, both to learn what progress had been made, but without betraying their true intent. Palacios left around ten o'clock, and Agnes told Basch that she believed that Palacios would go along, but she would not know until the morning.[33]

In later years, through rumor or folklore, this episode evolved into a sexual seduction, which more than anything else established Agnes's historical persona. According to one contemporary account, when the colonel refused the check, Agnes asked, "Isn't the sum enough?" At which point she began to undress. "Well, Colonel, here am I!" she reportedly exclaimed. The astonished Palacios tried to retreat, the story went, but finding the door locked he threatened to jump through the window when Agnes gave up and let him out. In a more general version, the reliable Sara Yorke Stevenson wrote, "Princess Salm-Salm cleverly used every means in a woman's power" to save Maximilian. While Agnes may well have used sex to advance her agenda, in this instance at least she apparently did not. Dr. Basch wrote that "a few minutes before ten o'clock I reached the princess's house, where I found both colonels." As Agnes clearly expected Basch, she most likely would not have engaged in sexual activity with either of her guests.[34]

Things moved quickly now. Palacios went directly to General Escobedo and gave up the foreign conspirators, but not Villanueva. The next morning Agnes found a guard posted at her door. Dr. Basch gained admittance with a pass but on leaving was arrested. Soon a carriage arrived to take Agnes to Escobedo's headquarters. The general, she recalled, "looked black as a thunderstorm." Escobedo observed sarcastically that Querétaro did not seem to agree with her and that she should go to San Luis Potosí, where she would be much healthier. She thanked the general but informed him that she never felt better and had no intention of leaving. At this, Escobedo lost his composure. According to Agnes, "He said he found it so extremely wrong in me, so against all feeling of gratitude and honour, that I, after he had shown me so much kindness and treated me so well, tried to bribe his officers and to bring him into an embarrassing position." She countered that she had done nothing that he would not have done under similar circumstances. He did not disagree but still insisted that she leave and that all of the ministers receive the same order. When Agnes protested that Maximilian required their services, Escobedo responded, "What good . . . can such old Women be to a man? Pretty people are these ministers! Two of them have already run away without even waiting for their baggage."[35]

Agnes left Escobedo's headquarters determined to stay, but soon a carriage arrived at her house to take her away. When a captain took her arm to escort her, Agnes claimed, "As quick as lightening, I drew from under my dress my little revolver, and pointing it at the breast of the horrified captain, I cried, 'Captain, touch me with one finger and you are a dead man!' The poor captain protested that he only followed orders. Finally, Agnes relented, packed her things, and with Jimmy and her servant boarded the carriage. She requested permission to see her husband, which Escobedo refused, but an officer scribbled a note that he sent to Salm. The captain then informed her that they would go first to Escobedo, which Agnes absolutely refused to do. Colonel Villanueva intervened. He went to the general for a change of orders. The colonel later related to Salm, "The general laughed, and said that he would rather stand opposite a whole Imperial battalion than meet the angry Princess Salm."[36]

Salm spent an anxious morning of June 14; he knew nothing of the previous night's events. A cryptic note delivered that afternoon by an Indian woman informed him that his wife had been sent away. Later in the day the officer of the guard came for Salm, telling him that the plot had been discovered, and, as he had been warned of the consequences, he knew what to expect. Salm was isolated from the other prisoners and denied visitors, but Colonel Villanueva, who avoided discovery (or had been working under orders all along), arrived to fill in the details: the princess had been sent under guard to San Luis Potosí; Dr. Basch had been locked up but was permitted to see the emperor in order to settle his affairs. On June 16 Salm learned that the court-martial had ended in a verdict of death for Maximilian, Mejía, and Miramón. Villanueva came with news that the verdict had indeed been rendered and confirmed by General Escobedo. The three men were to be shot that afternoon. Salm asked if any hope remained, to which the colonel replied, "None whatever; at three o'clock everything will be over." But Agnes had one more card to play.[37]

CHAPTER 6

All the Kings and Queens of Europe

Agnes might have been an unprincipled adventuress or, as ladies in Mexico called her, a *soldadera,* but as Sara Yorke Stevenson accurately observed, "she and her husband bravely stood by the Emperor to the bitter end, when older and more valued, though less courageous, friends had dropped away, and had left him." Over the past several months Salm had become Maximilian's closest friend. Now they were separated, never to see each other again. And a tender relationship developed between Agnes and the emperor that could not have been the product of her ambition. At some point a genuine bond developed that compelled her to risk her own life, just as her husband had done repeatedly, for the sake of a man who under different circumstances likely would not have received her. Agnes, it was believed, became the only woman that he allowed near him after learning of Carlota's madness. Perhaps she filled a void during those excruciating days of confinement; maybe he found in her something of his wife's spirit. Whatever the case, as others waited for the end to come, Agnes tried once more to save Maximilian's life.[1]

By the time Agnes reached San Luis Potosí, Maximilian had been condemned to death. Still, she would not give up. She went at once to see President Juárez, who could not see her but sent Minister of Justice José María Iglesias to deal with the excited woman. Iglesias, a gifted administrator and politician, had assisted Agnes during her previous visits and had listened to her emotional pleadings. He did so again, but when Agnes insisted upon seeing the president, he told her to return later. When she did, Agnes found Juárez friendly but largely unyielding. He told her that he knew about her activities and that she would have to remain in San Luis Potosí—under surveillance. He told her, too, that he could not spare Maximilian's life, but she could rest assured that should Salm be sentenced to death he would not be executed. On this, Agnes maintained, "he gave me his hand and his word of honour." With that, she surrendered—for the time being.[2]

Juárez had ordered the execution postponed to June 19, only after the doomed men had taken last rites and prepared to die. Appeals to Juárez poured into San Luis Potosí from around the world. United States Secretary of State Seward, Italian patriot Giuseppe Garibaldi, French novelist Victor Hugo, all sympathetic to the Republican government, pleaded for clemency, along with most of the European monarchies. Several leading Mexican liberals, including even Generals Escobedo and Porfirio Díaz, recommended that Maximilian be spared. Then, of course, there were the women like Agnes, and Miramón's pretty young wife, who brought her children before the president. But Juárez had learned a painful lesson about leniency, and he intended to send a message to the world.[3]

"I was like one distracted during all that time," Agnes wrote, "and day and night I revolved in my head how the Emperor might still be saved." Her main hope consisted of gaining yet another delay so that she could ask President Johnson, "whom [she] knew well," to send a "more energetic" protest. Both Iglesias and Juárez insisted that there would be no more delays. Still, on the night before the scheduled execution, Agnes tried one last time. According to her, the president received her readily. "With trembling lips," she recalled, "I pleaded for the life of the Emperor." But Juárez refused to comply—he would not prolong Maximilian's agony any longer. Agnes then performed another act for which she earned a place in history:

When I heard these cruel words I became frantic with grief. Trembling in every limb and sobbing, I fell down on my knees, and pleaded with words which came from my heart, but which I cannot remember. The President tried to raise me, but I held his knees convulsively, and said I would not leave him before he had granted his life. I saw the President was moved; he as well as Mr. Iglesia had tears in their eyes, but he answered me with a low, sad voice, "I am grieved, madame, to see you thus on your knees before me; but if all the kings and queens of Europe were in your place I could not spare that life. It is not I who take it, it is the people and the law; and if I should not do its will the people would take it and mine also."

The melodrama continued: "In my raving agony I exclaimed, he might take my life if blood was wanted." Finally, the president raised her from her knees and told her that her husband would be spared; but that was it. Agnes thanked him and took her leave.[4]

On the bright, beautiful morning of June 19, 1867, time ran out. Maximilian, Mejía, and Miramón, surrounded by elite formations of Republican troops, boarded separate carriages for the excruciating ride to El Cerro de las Campanas, where they were shot before a firing squad. Of the foreigners still in Querétaro, only Baron Magnus, two German merchants, and Maximilian's Hungarian cook Tudos witnessed the event. Salm and Basch remained locked in their cells. Despite the fact that the world had been warned, the execution nonetheless sent shock waves through the United States and Europe—the barbarous Mexicans had killed a Hapsburg prince. But it had been only a small act of retribution for centuries of exploitation. Maximilian, who truly wanted to do well by Mexico, became simply an unfortunate example. His death, sadly, did nothing to end Mexico's suffering or its exploitation. With the empire dead and the conservatives discredited, it would not be long before the victorious Republicans began to fight among themselves.

For now, Salm's ordeal continued. He remained confined, awaiting trial. He took the news of the execution badly and obsessed over his own escape. Other news came: on June 20, Mexico City fell to Porfirio Díaz. Márquez, who had ruled the city severely in the name of Maximilian, went into hiding and eventually escaped to Cuba, but Vidaurri, whose betrayal of Juárez guaranteed death, was captured and executed in a most degrading fashion. General Díaz, soon to challenge Juárez for the presidency, quickly released the foreign officers and sent them on to Europe. Salm was not the only one who believed that had Maximilian surrendered to Díaz he would not have been executed. Of course, such beliefs brought little consolation, and Salm's anxiety grew acute.[5]

Agnes suffered too, albeit in much more comfortable surroundings. She got the dreaded news at San Luis Potosí, after which she wrote to her husband, asking him to seek Escobedo's authorization for her to return to Querétaro. He did as requested, and Agnes received her release. She arrived at the former Imperial bastion in the first days of July to find Salm thin, pale, and excitable. He refused to believe that the president promised to spare his life—he could not trust the word of Juárez, whom he called "the blood-thirsty Indian," and still believed that he would be shot. He claimed that during this reunion Agnes slipped him a loaded revolver. If so, she did not acknowledge the act, and Salm never used the gun. While Salm harbored nothing but hatred toward his captors, Agnes proved much more introspective: "At that time I was of course furious against General Escobedo; but if I consider what I attempted to do, and that I was by no means yielding, I must acknowledge that I was treated throughout with great forbearance and courtesy, not only by General Escobedo, but also by Mr. Juarez[,] his minister, and by all Mexicans with whom I came in contact." But her presence made escape that much more difficult, as authorities increased guards and paid closer attention. After a few days, Agnes moved on to Mexico City, where, she believed, she could do her husband more good. But Salm would not be alone in prison; Jimmy the dog stayed behind to keep him company.[6]

The day after Agnes left, July 13, Salm and the remaining imprisoned officers went on trial. He, like his emperor before him, refused to attend the proceedings. Nor was his presence required. The whole affair took only three days. On July 17, a staff officer announced the sentence: all of the accused were to be shot on the afternoon of July 19. Salm, having not heard from Agnes, prepared for death. He arranged with a local apothecary for the embalming of his body and, on the night before his scheduled execution, he met with a priest, who would administer last rites the following morning. "After he had gone," Salm wrote, "I ordered the Caboquarto [corporal of the guard] to bring me writing paper, wine, and cigars, and wrote, until two o'clock A.M., letters to my wife, my brother, and other relatives and friends." These tasks completed, he went to sleep, quite sure that he would be dead in a matter of hours. He rose early, shaved, and then received Ricardo Villanueva, to whom he entrusted a packet of letters addressed to Agnes. He asked the friendly colonel to take care of Jimmy until she returned. It seemed that executions rarely went off as scheduled in Querétaro, and true to form, a staff officer soon arrived to announce a five-day delay—hardly a comforting respite in light of earlier experiences.[7]

On July 22, the Mexican government postponed the execution indefinitely. In August, Salm and the rest of the officers learned that execution no longer figured in their futures. New punishments ranged from two to ten years in prison; Salm got seven. Agnes, who supposedly had been working on her husband's behalf in Mexico City, arrived at Querétaro on September 8. Eventually, Salm enjoyed liberalized visitation privileges, and Agnes spent a good deal of time with him. He even received permission to walk about the city. In October the captives learned that they would be split up and sent to various prisons around Mexico, some to Veracruz, some south to Oaxaca, and some to Piedras Negras on the Rio Grande. Salm requested that he be sent to Oaxaca—in Porfirio Díaz's zone of control. The prisoners bound for Veracruz and Oaxaca headed toward Mexico City; Agnes followed in a coach. At the capital, the men went into temporary confinement, while Agnes worked for her husband's release or at least to have him sent to Veracruz, which, Salm admitted, "offered more chances for escape," and also fell under Díaz's administrative jurisdiction.[8]

Salm finally got the chance to meet the man who had become, it appeared, something of a champion to him—Porfirio Díaz. On the last day of October the prisoners departed Mexico City for their respective destinations. At Tehuacán, southeast of Puebla, they came to the headquarters of General Díaz. According to Salm, a staff officer retained him, saying that Díaz would arrive shortly and would "be pleased to make my acquaintance." Writing in 1868, Salm proved prophetic when he estimated that Díaz "will certainly still play an important part in the history of Mexico, and probably become its president." But the author did not have a totally accurate grasp on the gifted general and politician: "had not his noble character and patriotism checked his ambition, he might have made himself president by force of arms." The general greeted Salm cordially, offered him a room in his home, and had his horses stabled. The prince dined that evening with Díaz but begged off the offer of a room to stay with his comrades. On November 3, as the prisoners prepared to leave—for Oaxaca or Veracruz—Salm thanked Díaz for his hospitality. The general presented Salm with letters of recommendation to the commander at Veracruz.[9]

Salm headed to his next destination, feeling better about his situation. At Córdoba, he received a telegram from Agnes; her efforts had at last borne fruit—the president had signed his release. Agnes had been working the diplomatic circles, she claimed, writing to her "friend" President Johnson, who "caused Mr. Seward to write a private letter to Mr. Juarez in reference to the Prince." She also enlisted the assistance of Admiral Wilhelm von Tegetthoff of the Austrian fleet, who on the sad errand to bring Maximilian's body back to his family had been delayed by repeated refusals to release the remains. Baron Magnus, who continued to represent Prussian interests, still worked for Salm's release. For whatever reason or by what influence, the Mexican government agreed to free the prince. Magnus left for Veracruz with the signed release during the first week of November. Why Agnes did not go with him she did not say.[10]

Salm arrived at Veracruz expecting to receive his freedom, but his ordeal continued. The officer to whom he reported had no information about a release and insisted that Salm and the other prisoners be taken to the old Spanish fortress of San Juan d'Ulloa, located on an island off Veracruz. There they found themselves assigned to dank casemates, with very little to eat. Salm never had faith in the promises of Juárez and his ministers—the vindictive Mexicans never intended to free him—so immediately he began to plan his escape. Plenty of ships always waited in the waters off the deadly coast. Then, on November 13, word reached him that Baron Magnus had delivered his release. Once free and ashore, Salm called on Magnus to thank him; he then sent a telegram to Agnes, who would arrive in four days. Together they would sail for Europe. But things never seemed to go as planned for the Salm-Salms in Mexico. The commander at Veracruz told Salm that he must sail at once on a ship that also carried Magnus, Blasio, and several other players in the tragedy. He only could leave Agnes a letter, asking her to follow him as soon as she could. That done, he sailed for home. "On the 24th of December, [1867]," the prince recalled, "I was in the castle of my brother, in Anholt, and spent a merry Christmas with my family, which I had not been able to do for many long years."[11]

Strangely, Salm finished his memoir of Mexico without mentioning that Agnes indeed joined him in Europe, but not in time for the Christmas celebration. "My despair may be imagined," she wrote of her arrival at Veracruz. She missed her husband by a day. Not waiting for her baggage, she booked passage on the first ship available. The vessel was not bound for Europe. The princess went instead to New Orleans and from there on to New York. After updating her wardrobe for cold weather, she traveled to Washington, where she visited her sister and, she claimed, President Johnson, to thank him for his assistance. Then it was back to New York. She sailed for Brest, France, on December 28, 1867. Her journey across the Atlantic brought more tribulations, as she apparently had to hide her twenty-pound, long-legged terrier. "A baby," she wrote, "may be shown openly—and this is rather the pleasant side of baby transportation—conductors cannot object; whilst a dog must be carefully concealed. . . . If Jimmy could write his memoirs his book would be read with great sympathy, not only by the whole canine tribe, but also by all ladies who cherish a four-legged pet." Salm met her in Paris, and together they arrived at Schloss Anholt on January 11, 1868, thus the princess at last found her castle.[12]

"More I Do Not Desire"

If Agnes and Felix believed, which they most likely did not, that Europe promised a respite from almost six years of fairly constant adventure, they soon found otherwise. After a brief period of rest, during which Salm fretted over his future, the couple traveled to Vienna, hoping that Emperor Franz Josef would reward their faithful service to his brother with a commission in the Austrian army. But the emperor had been overburdened by claimants from Mexico and showed little appreciation or sympathy. Agnes had better luck with Maximilian's mother, Archduchess Sophie, who thanked her with a small annuity.[13]

In Europe, they found nothing of the hero's welcome they might have expected, and before long Salm's old creditors came calling. To make matters worse, they accumulated more debt fulfilling the social obligations, and Agnes battled poor health and depression. Still, they bounced around Germany, attending parties and dining with other minor royalty. To avoid relentless creditors and in search of some peace and quiet, they retreated to Switzerland's Lake Constance area, where Salm completed his book, *My Diary in Mexico,* which was published in German and English in the fall of 1868. In October they moved on to Berlin in an attempt to find employment with the mighty Prussian army.

This time Salm was not disappointed. King Wilhelm I received him graciously and soon had him commissioned a major in the Fourth Guards Regiment, the "Queen Augusta" Regiment. The step down in rank did not seem to bother him. After all, this was the Prussian army. That December, Queen Augusta received Felix and Agnes, offering the princess her first introduction to a queen. At Berlin and at Koblenz, the home of the queen's regiment, the Salm-Salms found themselves in the upper echelons of German society. They encountered Otto von Bismarck—like Porfirio Díaz, destined for a much larger role on the world stage—Czar Alexander II of Russia, and most of the important princes and princesses of Germany and Austria, not to mention dozens of barons and baronesses, counts and countesses, dukes and duchesses. In 1869 they settled in Koblenz and began again to enjoy life.

War between Prussia and France loomed—it was only a matter of time. With Queen Augusta's blessing, Agnes rekindled her interest in the care of sick and wounded soldiers. She did not wish to be a nurse but a surgeon's assistant. And to this end, she studied under an eminent German surgeon. After the declaration of war reached Berlin in July, 1870, Agnes secured authorization to accompany the doctor as a hospital assistant. So as Salm marched with his regiment, Agnes followed the army in an official capacity, and when fighting began she rendered valuable service. But her professional satisfaction was interrupted by news from the front.

As he watched the French troops evacuate Mexico City, chanting "on to Berlin," Salm had hoped that he could be there to meet them. The French never made it to Berlin, but Salm got his wish when Prussian armies pushed into France in the summer of 1870. West of the walled city of Metz, the same Marshal Bazaine who led those Frenchmen out of Mexico placed his army of some 115,000 in the path of two Prussian armies that numbered almost 190,000 together. On August 18 the Prussians struck the French line at Gravelotte and St. Privat (south and north, respectively). Both positions were well defended, but at St. Privat the German commander pushed the Guards Corps, including Salm's regiment, ahead against the rapid-firing French. Within minutes, 8,000 Prussians fell killed and wounded. Major Prince Salm, advancing on horseback, made an easy target. Quickly, a bullet shattered his right arm. Unhorsed, he advanced on foot until shot through the breast and again in the leg. Removed from the field, he died later that night. The Prussians prevailed as Bazaine proved unequal to the task at hand. That much, at least, afforded Salm's death a certain poetic justice.[14]

Agnes received the news three days later. She, along with her brother-in-law Prince Alfred, retrieved the prince's body and took it to Anholt for burial. Alfred asked her to stay with the family, but she returned to her duties with the army and served until the end of the brief conflict. Her work garnered much praise; she received letters of thanks from two high-ranking generals. And, she claimed, General Edwin von Manteuffel nominated her for the coveted Iron Cross, one of the most prized decorations in the world. But the Iron Cross only went to men—she would receive the highest decoration available to women and civilians.

After the war, Agnes found herself in dire financial condition. She could not cover Salm's debts, even with some help from his family, and her health soon deteriorated. She settled in Bonn but continued to travel. Yet she had lost her direction, perhaps even her will to live, and suffered the humiliation of indebtedness that would not go away.

There seemed to be no place for a beautiful twenty-eight-year-old widowed princess with three wars under her belt. During a trip to Italy in 1872, she decided on a desperate change—to enter a convent. But Agnes could not seek the advice of a priest or even a bishop—she had to see the pope. She wrote to Queen Augusta for a letter of introduction, which, according to Agnes, she provided. The princess claimed to have had two audiences with Pope Pius IX, who informed her accurately that she lacked "a vocation for a nunnery," no doubt sparing the Church a small scandal.

Agnes retreated to her rented house at Bonn on the Rhine to re-evaluate life again. Finally, good fortune returned in the form of a letter from America. It seemed that a distant relative, whom she had only met once as a child, admired young Agnes's spirit and had followed her career in the papers. Upon his death, he left her a sizable inheritance. With that Agnes settled in Europe for good. She bought a modest house in Bonn, where she remained for a number of years. When she published her *Ten Years of My Life* in 1876, Jimmy was still around. She closed her book with hopeful words: "I have a home with which I am perfectly satisfied, am independent in every respect, and have some true friends who know and love me; more I do not desire." That year she married a minor English diplomat named Charles Heneage, but the marriage dissolved quickly. She remained Princess Salm-Salm. At some point, Agnes moved to Karlsruhe. Thanks to her inheritance and her pension from the Hapsburgs, she lived in comfortable retirement, traveling and entertaining friends.[15]

In 1899, after an absence of more than thirty years, Agnes returned to the United States, bearing the colors of Salm's Civil War regiments, flags that, like Agnes, somehow managed to survive.

Epilogue

More Than a Woman's Part

Agnes found America in 1899 much changed. Its population of some seventy-five million people had almost doubled since she left, and eight new states had entered the union, bringing the total to forty-five. Only a year before, the United States had made quick work of a crumbling Spanish empire to take its place among the world's great powers, occupying Cuba, Puerto Rico, and the Philippines. Possessing a rejuvenated navy and plans for further expansion, the United States readied itself for an even greater role in the world. Although she did not visit, Agnes might have learned that under the dictatorship of Porfirio Díaz, Mexico had experienced more than twenty years of unprecedented stability.

In New York City, wide, paved boulevards covered Manhattan Island; the great Brooklyn Bridge linked Manhattan and the burgeoning city across the East River. Electric lights, trams, and telephones now served the area. Metropolitan New York boasted a population of three million people. And Washington had begun to resemble more the seat of a great nation. Mostly gone were the muddy streets and roving livestock that Agnes encountered on her first visit to the capital.

The people of United States now celebrated and romanticized the recent past, a past to which Agnes belonged, even if sometimes only in legend. During the time of her visit, Pawnee Bill's Wild West Show, which offered up the noble Indian stereotype, toured New Jersey, while the Ringling Brothers' Circus played Chicago. Civil War veterans continued to gather, and each year the stories got more glorious and less gruesome.[1]

Agnes enjoyed wonderful receptions in New York City, Vineland, Chicago, and Des Moines, but things had changed in a more personal way for Agnes. During a stop at Washington, she called upon President William McKinley, expecting, no doubt, the reception she once enjoyed. She sent in her card, as was her habit, only to be told that the president had no time to see her. But at New York, she knew that she could still attract a crowd.[2]

On May 14 Agnes arrived at Odd Fellows' Hall on East Eighth Street in New York City. She came to present the flags of her husband's former Civil War regiments to the surviving veterans. "The Princess took her place near the stage," the *New York Times* reported. "She was dressed in a black silk gown with a long train and a small black hat fringed with pink roses. There was a red ribbon over her shoulder, and on her breast were medals of gold which had been presented to her for bravery on the field of battle."

In attendance were such dignitaries as General Julius Stahel, one-time commander of the 8th New York Infantry; U.S. Senator Carl Schurz, a former Union general and a prominent German-American; and Agnes's friend S. H. M. Byers, author of the poem "Sherman's March to the Sea," who had hosted her in Des Moines. Mostly, the crowd consisted of the survivors of the 8th Regiment and their families.

Agnes presented the flag to the survivors with a brief speech: "This flag came into my possession from my husband, who was one of your comrades. It has been a pleasant duty for me to cherish it for nearly thirty-five years, and now I present it to you, in memory of my husband." General Stahel, who had once endorsed a protest of Salm's appointment, toasted Agnes. Schurz, an old Forty-eighter himself, recalled for the audience the times when he watched the valiant charges of the 8th at

Chancellorsville and Gettysburg—until one of the veterans reminded him that the regiment had quit the war before those battles took place. The veterans proclaimed Agnes "the Mother of the Regiment," even if she were only eighteen years old when they mustered out. The rich irony of the event escaped notice. The old soldiers had, it appeared, forgotten that many of them had hated the boastful young beauty and her aristocrat husband. Still, it must have been a glorious day.[3]

On June 5, the princess attended two more receptions in her honor at Newark, New Jersey, and New York City. The next day she boarded a trans-Atlantic steamer for Europe. On June 24, the Vineland *Evening Journal* reported that Agnes had cabled from South Hampton, England, to say that she had arrived safely and enjoyed a pleasant voyage. From England, she traveled to her home at Karlsruhe on the Rhine. She returned to America in 1900 to raise funds for relief work associated with South Africa's Boer War, and in May she attended a dinner in her honor at the Hotel Manhattan, but this trip passed without the fanfare of her previous visit.[4]

Agnes continued to entertain visitors at her mountain home in Germany, and in 1902, she hosted the famous humanitarian and founder of the American Red Cross, Clara Barton, with whom she maintained a lively correspondence. Agnes also enjoyed the presence of her young niece and namesake, Agnes Winona Johnson (daughter of her sister Della), who spent much time with her aunt in Europe.[5]

Princess Agnes Salm-Salm died at Karlsruhe on December 21, 1912. Her obituary ran in such papers as the *Times* of London and the *New York Times*. The London paper noted that "Princess Agnes took more than a woman's part" in the American Civil War, "being not only a skilled nurse, but a horsewoman of great daring and, apparently, a most energetic and successful recruiting agent." In the Franco-Prussian War, the British obituary continued, "Princess Agnes was `attached' to the Army staff as a mounted officer." The *New York Times* reported that she had been born in Baltimore, the daughter of an "American Colonel named Leclercq," and "in her youth gained some renown as an actress." Even in death she spawned fiction. Agnes was buried in Bonn, next to Miss Louise Runkel, a close friend with whom she worked during the Franco-Prussian War.[6] Whether Agnes chose her simple interment or had perhaps been denied the chance to rest beside her prince went unreported.

By 1899, at least to the people who cared to notice, Agnes Salm-Salm represented a heroine of dime-novel proportions. However, she never led troops in battle, nor did she march with Sherman to the sea; she did not win the Iron Cross, nor was she a close friend of President Lincoln. She never performed in the theater or, most likely, in the circus. She did, though, meet or know four emperors, three presidents, one future president, and a host of other important figures; she had an uncanny ability to influence powerful men to her advantage and that of her husband. And she tried, at least more than anyone on the scene, to save Maximilian from the firing squad. Finally, when she had little to gain and nothing to prove, she worked tirelessly in the hospitals of the Franco-Prussian War.

Whether or not her efforts represented an expansion of the traditional role of women in the nineteenth century is beside the point. Her title placed her in a position of privilege and afforded her a stage, which was more than most women could expect. She lived life with a dash and daring that inspired both admiration and ridicule. Yet she also matured in the crucible of danger and personal loss that characterized her post–Civil War life and went on to do genuine good in the field hospitals of Europe before fading into obscurity. Regrettably, the fiction that surrounds her early life and her wartime adventures—relatively minor compared to legends of the "Wild West" and largely fostered by Agnes herself—obscures the real person and her real experiences, which were, by any measure, remarkable.

APPENDIX A

The Writings of Prince and Princess Salm-Salm

According to the prince, included among Emperor Maximilian's numerous last requests was a wish that Felix work with other survivors of his inner circle to write a history of the Mexican Empire, one no doubt that reflected favorably on the emperor. Despite vigorous attempts to gain access to Hapsburg records, Salm found his efforts blocked by Maximilian's family, who wanted nothing more to do with the failed enterprise. He nonetheless resolved to record at least that portion of the emperor's life that he shared. The result became *My Diary in Mexico in 1867, Including the Last Days of the Emperor Maximilian; with Leaves from the Diary of the Princess Salm-Salm,* published in two volumes at Stuttgart in 1868. Later that year publisher Richard Bentley & Son of London released an English translation. Excerpts of the book also appeared in Spanish and French.

Salm's work is a detailed, colorful, and valuable account of his experiences in Mexico—an important contribution to the historical record. And it is considered credible. Salm's style is matter-of-fact, and his tone, while certainly gallant, is not self-aggrandizing. The book is all that Maximilian could have desired. As one might expect, it reflects positively on the emperor and many of those who served him loyally to the end, but Salm pulls no punches in his indictment of Colonel Lopez, whom he condemns for his role in Maximilian's capture, or those who failed Maximilian in one way or another. Salm's book includes letters and documents in addition to Agnes's contribution.

The so-called leaves from Princess Salm-Salm's diary do not appear as such. Her contribution is a running narrative that may have been derived from a diary that she claimed to have kept. Interestingly, the prince and princess do not always agree on the recollection of events in which they both participated.

Still, Salm's work, including Agnes's "diary," has been cited copiously in almost all historical treatments of the Mexican Empire.

Four years after the publication of Salm's *My Diary in Mexico,* after the Franco-Prussian War changed the Western world, and after the death of her husband in that war, Agnes found the time to write her memoir of the ten momentous years she spent with the prince. By then she knew of the wild tales she had already inspired. "It would, indeed," she wrote, "be cruel and ungrateful to novelists and dramatic poets, who have made me the heroine of their most wonderful and fanciful works, to disenchant their public!" She dismissed the need to address these literary inventions by informing her readers that she would convey only her experiences and observations from the years 1862 to 1872. This would be no autobiography.

As with her contribution to Salm's work (which, almost unaltered, forms the bulk of her own chapters on Mexico), she claimed to have relied on "a carefully and regularly kept diary" as well as "a very good memory." Regrettably, her diary has never surfaced.

And like Salm's earlier effort, Agnes's two-volume *Ten Years of My Life* was first published in Germany, before Richard Bentley & Son of London released an English-language version in 1876. But similarities end there. *Ten Years of My Life* lacks the narrative elegance of Salm's *Diary,* and it possesses a much more self-interested approach. It also reflects the author's naiveté and narrow grasp of reality. In short, it reads much like the work of a young, inexperienced American woman thrust into the role of a European princess. Her style is awkward and unimaginative; her tone is often haughty, uncouth, and insensitive, perhaps an ineffective attempt to affect the voice of royalty. Still, according to later reports, the book sold reasonably well in Europe and the United States.

New York Times *Review* *of* Ten Years of My Life, *April 2, 1877*

The Princess Salm-Salm appears to be chiefly remarkable for following in the steps of Florence Nightingale. She imbibed a taste for war and the Sanitary Commission during the rebellion, when Salm-Salm came over to get pay and glory in the army of the North and to woo and win his Princess. The latter has a straightforward and rather artless mode of expressing herself. She begins before she had met her Prince, with her return from Cuba in the Fall of 1861, describes her journey to Washington and a comical review of the Union cavalry. After that come descriptions of the German regiments and their commanders, her meeting with Salm-Salm, and their marriage. In the same hurried and artless style of journal-making, we get various accounts of spiritualistic séances, of the admirable contrivances used for the sick in the Union Army, gossip about Commander-in-Chief, and all the rest of the ordinary events of which one might expect to hear. An amusing tone is given by her frank avowal of the measures she took, the personal lobbying she engaged in, to get her husband advanced in grade. One feels at once that her acquaintance with America and Americans is as superficial as it well could be. The part devoted to the rebellion is finished in 122 pages. Of Lincoln she speaks in affectionate terms, but her estimate of Grant is by no means flattering. When she states that he was a General of no genius, but merely possessed of shrewdness and tenacity, she probably re-echoes the opinion of Salm-Salm and the German officers who seem to have been his chief companions. She mentions quite naturally the reason for Salm-Salm's appearance in the United States: he was so persecuted by his creditors that flight was the only alternative to arrest. After the Mexican campaign, when Felix goes to Vienna, in hopes that the Emperor will reward the faithful officer of Maximilian with some office, he is hunted down by his creditors, and gets away by paying cash down to the bailiff. Then a wily creditor offers to conceal him on his own premises against all others, but even that will not do. Prince Felix has to decamp. The events in Mexico which ended in the death of Maximilian occupy something like another hundred pages, and are just as full of camp gossip as the preceding, the main difference being that the names have a more aristocratic sound, and the events are more dramatic. In the United States Felix would seem to have owed promotion chiefly to his energetic wife; in Mexico he owed her his life, for, to judge from her account, his life was spared chiefly because of letters written to Juarez by President Johnson, the Princess herself having written to the United States imploring his aid. She is deep in intrigues to save the life of the Emperor by flight from Mexico, but although her plans were easily discovered, she acknowledges that the Mexicans treated her with extreme leniency. The rest of the book is occupied with the Franco-German war, and an account of her introduction to the family of her husband in Germany, an account which is not unfeeling, because she seems to have no ill will toward them, but at least blunt, and in rather poor taste. She writes of them as if she were not a relative, and under no obligations them. Her account of the hospitals and sanitary arrangements of the Prussian Army is interesting; she compares it unfavorably with the American ambulance system. The cool impudence with which she hits off the grandees of Prussia and Spain is very American, if not particularly edifying. There is evidently no Princess about her, saving only the name, and, doubtless, that very fact made her interesting to people unused to so much republican boldness. The portrait that faces the title page is that of an English woman, if it be possible to distinguish such nice shades of nationality. Readers will find the book a gossipy, superficial, and decidedly amusing performance.

NOTES

Preface

1. *(Des Moines) Iowa State Register,* May 4, 1899.
2. For a discussion of gender see Joan W. Scott's groundbreaking article "Gender: A Useful Category of Historical Analysis," *American Historical Review* 91 (Dec., 1986): 1053–75. See also two works by Elizabeth D. Leonard, *Yankee Women: Gender Battles in the Civil War* and *All the Daring of the Soldier: Women of the Civil War Armies.*
3. Richard Cohen, "The Lady Vanishes," *Washington Post Magazine,* Mar. 16, 1997, p. 10.

Introduction

1. *New York Times,* Apr. 5, 1899.
2. Ibid.
3. *Vineland (New Jersey) Evening Journal,* Apr. 6, 10, and 12, 1899.
4. Ibid., May 16, 1899; *(Des Moines) Iowa State Register,* Apr. 30, 1899.
5. Ibid., Apr. 30, 1899, May 4, 1899.
6. Ibid., May 4, 1899. According to her own memoir, *Ten Years of My Life,* Agnes was in and around her husband's camp at Bridgeport, Alabama, during Sherman's March. She met Byers not during the Civil War but when he served as U.S. consul at Zurich. See also William T. Sherman, *Memoirs of General William T. Sherman,* vol. 2, pp. 282–83; for Byers's meeting with Agnes in Europe see S. H. M. Byers, *Twenty Years in Europe,* pp. 310–11.
7. *(Des Moines) Iowa State Register,* May 5, 6, and 7, 1899.
8. *Vineland (New Jersey) Evening Journal,* May 25, May 31, June 1, 1899; Agnes Salm-Salm, Application for Membership, Daughters of the American Revolution, Number 28674, May 24, 1899, Daughters of the American Revolution National Headquarters, Washington, D.C., copy in author's possession.
9. *Le Courrier du Mexique (Mexico City),* June 11, 1899.

10. The Clara Barton Collection, Library of Congress, Washington, D.C.,
    includes several letters between Agnes Salm-Salm and Clara Barton.
    Much of the correspondence refers to Barton's visit to Salm-Salm's home
    in Germany. They address each other as "Sister." Agnes could have met
    Barton on several occasions—during the Civil War or the Franco-Prussian
    War—but she may well have made the acquaintance during her 1899 visit,
    because I found no correspondence between the two prior to 1900.

11. Agnes Salm-Salm, *Ten Years of My Life*, p. 4. All references to this work
    are from volume one unless otherwise indicated.

12. Ibid., pp. 3–5.

13. James R. Joy, *Thomas Joy and His Descendants*, pp. 90, 112, 142; *Dictionary of
    American Biography*, 1935 ed., s.v. "Salm-Salm, Agnes Elizabeth Winona
    Leclercq Joy," by J. R. Joy; Agnes Salm-Salm, *Ten Years of My Life*, p. 34;
    (Des Moines) Iowa State Register, Apr. 30, 1899, May 4, 1899. *Appletons' Cy-
    clopedia of American Biography*, 1888, s.v. "Salm-Salm, Felix." According to
    Joy, Agnes's sister Delilah (Della) was born in August, 1846, making a De-
    cember, 1845, birthrate for Agnes unlikely. Another sister, Emily, was born
    in August, 1843. 1840 and 1844 are both possible, but given her close rela-
    tionship with Della, 1844 appears a more likely year for Agnes's birth. On
    her DAR application, Agnes gave Swanton as her place of birth.

14. Frederick Otto Von Fritsch, *A Gallant Captain of the Civil War*, ed. Joseph
    Tyler Butts, p. 113; *Appletons' Cyclopedia of American Biography*, 1888, s.v.
    "Salm-Salm, Felix;" *New York Times*, Dec. 22, 1912.

15. *(Des Moines) Iowa State Register*, May 4, 1899.

16. Noah Brooks, *Washington in Lincoln's Time*, p. 69; Fritsch, *A Gallant Cap-
    tain*, p. 114; Blair Niles, *Passengers to Mexico: The Last Invasion of the Ameri-
    cans*, pp. 49–50. Niles provides one of the few extended secondary treat-
    ments of Agnes Salm-Salm, including a chapter titled "Circus-Rider
    Princess."

17. Ella Lonn, *Foreigners in the Union Army and Navy*, p. 566; *New York Times*,
    Dec. 22, 1912. Lonn's account is one of several secondary sources to advance
    the French lineage version. One would-be biographer developed the In-
    dian princess legend to ridiculous lengths, citing the name Winona as par-
    tial evidence of a Native-American heritage. See Florence Arms, *Bright
    Morning*.

18. Joy, *Thomas Joy and His Descendants*, contains a wealth of information on
    Agnes's family; her DAR application, written in her own hand, includes
    abstracts from the Revolutionary War Archives in Boston, which indicates
    more than a passing interest on her part.

19. *(Des Moines) Iowa State Register*, May 4, 1899. According to Joy, *Thomas Joy
    and His Descendants*, p. 112, Mrs. Mendel was Agnes's sister, the former
    Sarah Anne Joy, who was not Mrs. Mendel until 1861; the sister Agnes
    visited in Washington was Delilah (Della), who married Edmund Johnson
    in 1861, when she was fifteen years old.

Chapter 1

1. Agnes Salm-Salm, *Ten Years of My Life*, pp. 4–7. There are several useful studies of wartime Washington, including Brooks's *Washington in Lincoln's Time* and Margaret Leech, *Reveille in Washington, 1860–1865.*

2. Agnes Salm-Salm, *Ten Years of My Life*, pp. 7–8.

3. Ibid., pp. 8–15; William L. Burton, *Melting Pot Soldiers: The Union's Ethnic Regiments*, pp. 84–87; George B. McClellan, *McClellan's Own Story*, p. 142. Burton's excellent work is most useful on the politics of ethnicity in the Union Army. He presents a largely unfavorable impression of Felix Salm-Salm but credits Agnes's ingenuity.

4. McClellan, *McClellan's Own Story*, pp. 141–42; Agnes Salm-Salm, *Ten Years of My Life*, p. 10.

5. Ibid., p. 12.

6. Ibid., pp. 15–16.

7. *Appletons' Cyclopedia of America Biography*, 1888, s.v. "Salm-Salm, Felix"; *La Grande Encyclopédie* (France), s.v. "Salm"; Agnes Salm-Salm, *Ten Years of My Life*, p. 16; Franklin L. Ford, *Europe, 1780–1830*, 2d ed., pp. 212–14, 274.

8. Agnes Salm-Salm, *Ten Years of My Life*, pp. 17–18; Fritsch, *A Gallant Captain*, p. 114.

9. Agnes Salm-Salm, *Ten Years of My Life*, 18–19; *Harper's Weekly*, May 9, 1863; United States War Department, *War of the Rebellion: A Compilation of the Official Records of the Union and Confederate Armies*, hereafter cited as *OR*, series 3, vol. 1, pp. 528–29.

10. Burton, *Melting Pot Soldiers*, p. 87.

11. Agnes Salm-Salm, *Ten Years of My Life*, pp. 14, 19–20.

12. Robert G. Tanner, *Stonewall in the Valley: Thomas J. "Stonewall" Jackson's Shenandoah Valley Campaign, Spring 1862*, pp. 141, 294–95; Burton, *Melting Pot Soldiers*, pp. 88–89.

13. Agnes Salm-Salm, *Ten Years of My Life*, pp. 23, 25.

14. Felix Salm-Salm and Otto von Corvin to Abraham Lincoln, July 18, 1862, Abraham Lincoln Collection, Library of Congress; Agnes Salm-Salm, *Ten Years of My Life*, 56–59. A. E. Zucker, ed., *The Forty-Eighters: Political Refugees of the German Revolution of 1848*, p. 285. Agnes may have drafted the proposal as the handwriting resembles her own, but Corvin also spoke and wrote well in English. Both Agnes and Zucker claim that the plan was presented in 1863, but the dated documents in the Lincoln Collection show 1862.

15. Ibid., pp. 20–22; Fritsch, *A Gallant Captain*, pp. 113–14.

16. Agnes Salm-Salm, *Ten Years of My Life*, pp. 26–27; Stewart Sifakis, *Who Was Who in the Union*, pp. 179–80. Harris (1802–75) served only one term in the Senate. His daughter Clara was Major Henry Rathbone's date when they accompanied the Lincolns to Ford's Theater and witnessed the president's assassination. She married Rathbone, who later went mad and

murdered her. It should be noted that Agnes's influential friends did not include prominent Germans such as Carl Schurz and Franz Sigel.

17. Agnes Salm-Salm, *Ten Years of My Life*, pp. 28–29; Ezra J. Warner, *Generals in Blue: Lives of the Union Commanders*, pp. 332–33; Adjutant General's Office, "Felix Salm-Salm File," RG 94, National Archives, hereafter cited as AGO, "Salm-Salm File."

18. Gustav Struve, *Das 8. Regiment N.Y. Freiwilliger und Prinz Felix Salm-Salm*, pp. 1–8; Burton, *Melting Pot Soldiers*, pp. 87–91.

19. Ibid. Burton writes that Agnes took action against those who worked against her husband's appointment and that evidence suggests that her "jealous machinations" blocked von Gilsa's promotion to brigadier general, a rank he never achieved although he led a brigade for most of the war. More likely, his performances at Chancellorsville and Gettysburg made a lasting impression on superiors. It is also important to note that Salm was not anathema to all Forty-eighters: his friend Corvin served a prison term for his role in the Baden uprising; and Blenker clearly held him in high regard.

20. Agnes Salm-Salm, *Ten Years of My Life*, pp. 33–34; *OR*, series 1, vol. 21, p. 935.

21. Agnes Salm-Salm, *Ten Years of My Life*, pp. 35–36.

22. Shelby Foote, *The Civil War, A Narrative: Fredericksburg to Meridian*, pp. 128–31; Stephen W. Sears, *Chancellorsville*, pp. 19–22.

23. Ibid.

24. Agnes Salm-Salm, *Ten Years of My Life*, pp. 36–38.

25. Ibid., pp. 38–39; Sears, *Chancellorsville*, pp. 54–82. The much-maligned Burnside accepted his demotion and served the Union faithfully for the balance of the war. Many of his critics were also reassigned, leaving Hooker a considerably different command structure than that under Burnside. Hooker thus became the fifth commander of the main Federal army in the East (following McDowell, McClellan, Pope, and Burnside) in less than two years.

26. Agnes Salm-Salm, *Ten Years of My Life*, pp. 39–40; W. A. Swanberg, *Sickles the Incredible*, pp. 142–43. Sickles (1819–1914) would lose a leg at Gettysburg and go on to be U.S. minister to Spain. He remained a controversial figure.

27. Agnes Salm-Salm, *Ten Years of My Life*, pp. 39–40; Regis de Trobriand, *Four Years with the Army of the Potomac*, p. 428; Charles S. Wainwright, *A Diary of Battle: The Personal Journals of Charles S. Wainwright*, ed. Allan Nevins, p. 175. Sifakis, *Who Was Who in the Union*, p. 133. Colonel J. E. Farnum (1824–79) was a colorful character. In spring, 1863, he commanded Sickles's former "Excelsior" Brigade in the III Corps, but earlier he went to Nicaragua with the filibusterer William Walker and in 1859 was arrested for slave trading.

28. Charles Francis Adams, *Charles Francis Adams, 1835–1915: An Autobiography*,

p. 161; James I. Robertson, Jr., ed., *The Civil War Letters of General Robert McAllister,* p. 283; Robert McAllister Papers, Rutgers, State University of New Jersey Archibald Stevens Alexander Library Special Collections and University Archives. The word "hooker" as a synonym for prostitute is commonly believed to have originated in reference to female visitors to General Hooker's headquarters. According to one source, the term originated with prostitutes who served industrial workers, longshoremen, and sailors at New York City's Corlear's Hook section in the 1830s. Edwin G. Burrows and Mike Wallace, *Gotham: A History of New York City to 1898,* p. 484. Perhaps Hooker's visitors widened the usage.

29. Joshua Lawrence Chamberlain, *The Passing of the Armies,* p. 311.

30. Julia Lorrilard Butterfield, ed., *A Biographical Memorial of General Daniel Butterfield, Including Many Addresses and Military Writings,* pp. 160–61; Brooks, *Washington in Lincoln's Time,* pp. 68–69; St. Clair A. Mulholland, *The Story of the 116th Regiment, Pennsylvania Volunteers in the War of the Rebellion,* ed. Lawrence Frederick Kohl, pp. 86–87.

31. Swanberg, *Sickles the Incredible,* pp. 175–76. It should be noted that none of the major biographies of Lincoln mention the kissing event or the reported exchange with Sickles.

32. *OR,* series 1, vol. 51, part 1, pp. 998–99.

33. Frederick H. Dyer, comp., *A Compendium of the War of the Rebellion,* p. 1408.

34. Agnes Salm-Salm, *Ten Years of My Life,* pp. 48–51.

35. Frank L. Byrne and Andrew T. Weaver, eds., *Haskell of Gettysburg: His Life and Civil War Papers,* p. 85. Haskell's italics. Haskell was killed in the 1864 Battle of Cold Harbor.

Chapter 2

1. Sears, *Chancellorsville,* pp. 432–33. Jackson was mortally wounded by his own troops as he reconnoitered for a continuation of the attack; he died eight days after the attack.

2. Agnes Salm-Salm, *Ten Years of My Life,* pp. 52–54.

3. Ibid., pp. 59–61. Blenker died in October, 1863.

4. Burrows and Wallace, *Gotham,* pp. 887–95.

5. Agnes Salm-Salm, *Ten Years of My Life,* pp. 64–68.

6. Ibid., p. 64.

7. Burrows and Wallace, *Gotham,* pp. 895–96. Some 119 people died in the riot and more than 1,000 were wounded. The draft never provided the manpower boost that the government sought.

8. Agnes Salm-Salm, *Ten Years of My Life,* pp. 69–71.

9. J. G. Bennett to Abraham Lincoln, Oct. 26, 1863, Mrs. H. W. Bennett to Abraham Lincoln, Oct. 26, 1863, Abraham Lincoln Collection, Library of Congress.

10. Agnes Salm-Salm, *Ten Years of My Life,* pp. 69, 71; George Brown Tindall with David E. Shi, *America: A Narrative History,* 3d ed., p. 486.

11. Agnes Salm-Salm, *Ten Years of My Life,* pp. 71–79.

12. *OR,* series 1, vol. 29, part 2, p. 126; series 1, vol. 30, part 1, pp. 40–47. Just when Salm received the offer is unclear. Regimental returns of the Army of the Potomac for August 31, 1863, listed Bourry as colonel of the 68th, but Steinhausen commanded the regiment during the Chattanooga Campaign of November.

13. Agnes Salm-Salm, *Ten Years of My Life,* pp. 80–83; Warner, *Generals in Blue,* pp. 162–63.

14. Agnes Salm-Salm, *Ten Years of My Life,* pp. 83–84; Commission Records, 1863–65, Illinois State Archives; Richard Yates Correspondence, RS 101.013, Illinois State Archives; Richard Yates Papers, Manuscript Collection, Illinois State Historical Society. See also John H. Krenkell, ed., *Richard Yates: Civil War Governor.* Agnes does not appear in the extant Yates papers, nor is there a commission in her name, although the register contains many apparently honorary commissions.

15. Mary Elizabeth Massey, *Bonnet Brigades,* reissued as *Women in the Civil War,* pp. 68–71 [in either volume; pagination is the same].

16. See Leonard, *Yankee Woman.* Mary Walker served as a contract surgeon during the war. Her attempts to acquire an army commission never bore fruit. The United States created the Medal of Honor early in the war to recognize the meritorious acts of enlisted personnel, later extended eligibility to officers.

17. Bruce Catton, *The Army of the Potomac: A Stillness at Appomattox,* pp. 33–34; *OR,* series 1, vol. 32, part 1, pp. 11, 25–26, 32; *OR,* series 1, vol. 32, part 3, pp. 472, 560. Hooker's XX Corps was created mainly by combining the former XI and XII Corps.

18. Agnes Salm-Salm, *Ten Years of My Life,* pp. 101–102; Fritsch, *A Gallant Captain,* pp. 106–107; Frederick Phisterer, comp., *New York in the War of the Rebellion, 1861–1865,* 3d ed., vol. 3, p. 2673. Fritsch offers the best account of the 68th's activities, but his negative treatment of Salm, like Agnes's positive portrayal, must be weighed against other evidence when possible.

19. *OR,* series 1, vol. 32, part 3, p. 560; *OR,* series 1, vol. 39, part 2, pp. 63, 327. For a concise treatment of the Atlanta Campaign see David Coffey, *John Bell Hood and the Struggle for Atlanta.*

20. Agnes Salm-Salm, *Ten Years of My Life,* pp. 101–102.

21. Fritsch, *A Gallant Captain,* pp. 111–15.

22. Agnes Salm-Salm, *Ten Years of My Life,* 103–10.

23. Ibid., 110–11.

24. Fritsch, *A Gallant Captain,* 112–15. Fritsch made no secret of his infatuation with Agnes, and he hinted strongly that there was more to their relationship. This could account for his absence from her memoir.

25. Agnes Salm-Salm, *Ten Years of My Life,* pp. 113–14.

26. Ibid., pp. 120–25; Fritsch, *A Gallant Captain,* pp. 118–19.

27. *OR,* series 1, vol. 45, part 1, pp. 508, 513, 515–18, 521, 545, 801–802, 1126.

28. Agnes Salm-Salm, *Ten Years of My Life,* pp. 127–29. For Generals Brannan, Granger, and Meagher see Warner, *Generals in Blue,* pp. 42–43, 182, 317–18. Meagher (pronounced "Marr") was an interesting man and a likely associate for Agnes, whom she probably got to know when both were around the Army of the Potomac. An Irish nationalist, he led the famed "Irish Brigade" through Fredericksburg. Considered a problem, he spent the balance of the war in rear-area assignments. As acting governor of the Montana territory, he drowned under mysterious circumstances in 1867.

29. Ibid., pp. 132–33.

Chapter 3

1. *OR,* series 1, vol. 45, part 1, pp. 551, 559, 591, 601; *OR,* series 1, vol. 49, part 1, pp. 10–12, 33, 39, 702, 797.

2. Agnes Salm-Salm, *Ten Years of My Life,* pp. 137–38; AGO, "Edmund Johnson File."

3. Agnes Salm-Salm, *Ten Years of My Life,* pp. 138–39; Fritsch, *A Gallant Captain,* p. 125.

4. Warner, *Generals in Blue,* pp. xv–xx.

5. Agnes Salm-Salm, *Ten Years of My Life,* pp. 142–44.

6. Ibid., pp. 144–46; AGO, "Felix Salm-Salm File"; Phisterer, *New York in the War,* p. 420.

7. Warner, *Generals in Blue,* pp. xvi–xix. Warner's introduction provides a valuable discussion of the Federal rank system for general officers, while an appendix lists all brevet rank generals. In the Federal armies it was possible for a Regular officer serving in the volunteer establishment to hold four ranks at the same time: substantive and brevet grades in the Regulars and substantive and brevet grades in the Volunteers.

8. E. B. Long with Barbara Long, *The Civil War Day by Day: An Almanac, 1861–1865,* pp. 670–76.

9. Agnes Salm-Salm, *Ten Years of My Life,* pp. 149–54.

10. Ibid., pp. 155–57; AGO, "Edmund Johnson File." Agnes's version of this event does not jibe with the other available source, Joy, *Thomas Joy and His Descendants,* p. 142. Joy lists Della's second child's birthday as January 27, 1865, before the Johnsons arrived at Bridgeport, and gives the child's name as George Edmund Johnson. Felix Salm-Salm Johnson, their third child, was born on January 9, 1867. The story makes little sense in light of the unstable nature of the Salm-Salms' life and, especially, Agnes's undisciplined lifestyle.

11. Agnes Salm-Salm, *Ten Years of My Life,* pp. 157–65; AGO, "Felix Salm-Salm File"; Phisterer, *New York in the War,* vol. 3, p. 2673.

12. AGO, "Edmund Johnson File"; Agnes Salm-Salm, *Ten Years of My Life,* p. 160.
13. Agnes Salm-Salm, *Ten Years of My Life,* pp. 165–67.
14. Fritsch, *A Gallant Captain,* p. 141.
15. Agnes Salm-Salm, *Ten Years of My Life,* pp. 167–69.
16. Ibid., pp. 169–70; Phisterer, *New York in the War,* vol. 3, p. 2673.
17. Agnes Salm-Salm, *Ten Years of My Life,* p. 171; Felix Salm-Salm, *My Diary in Mexico,* p. 1. All references from this source are from volume one of the two-volume set except when indicated.
18. Ibid., p. 2.

Chapter 4

1. Ibid., 2–3; Agnes Salm-Salm, *Ten Years of My Life,* 170–173.
2. For the Reform see Richard N. Sinkin, *The Mexican Reform, 1855–1876: A Study in Liberal Nation Building.* Also useful is Laurens Ballard Perry, *Juárez and Díaz: Machine Politics in Mexico.* For the general history of Mexico see Michael C. Meyer and William L. Sherman, *The Course of Mexican History,* 5th ed.
3. For the general history of the French intervention and the empire of Maximilian numerous sources are available. The main sources consulted for this chapter are Count Egon Corti, *Maximilian and Charlotte of Mexico,* a two-volume, comprehensive work from a European point of view; Joan Haslip, *The Crown of Mexico: Maximilian and His Empress Carlota,* a much more popular account; Bertita Harding, *Phantom Crown: The Story of Maximilian and Carlota of Mexico.*
4. Many conservative leaders joined the republican cause during the intervention. See Don M. Coerver, *The Porfirian Interregnum: The Presidency of Manuel González of Mexico, 1880–1884.*
5. For the Monroe Doctrine see Dexter Perkins, *A History of the Monroe Doctrine,* and Ernest R. May, *The Making of the Monroe Doctrine.*
6. A useful study of U.S. opposition to the French intervention and Maximilian's empire is Alfred Jackson Hanna and Kathryn Abbey Hanna, *Napoleon III and Mexico: American Triumph over Monarchy.* For Seward see Glyndon G. Van Deusen, *William Henry Seward.*
7. See Roy Morris, Jr., *Sheridan: The Life and Wars of General Phil Sheridan;* Philip H. Sheridan, *Personal Memoirs of P. H. Sheridan.*
8. Much has been made of former Confederates in Mexico, and while numerous prominent generals did go, they never constituted a major bloc of support for Maximilian. See Andrew Rolle, *The Lost Cause: The Confederate Exodus to Mexico.*
9. Felix Salm-Salm, *My Diary in Mexico,* pp. 3–4.
10. Agnes Salm-Salm, *Ten Years of My Life,* pp. 176–78.

11. Ibid., pp. 181–94.

12. Ibid., pp. 240–41; Felix Salm-Salm, *My Diary in Mexico,* pp. 4–5.

13. Ibid., p. 5; Agnes Salm-Salm, *Ten Years of My Life,* pp. 242–43.

14. Ibid., pp. 243–44.

15. Felix Salm-Salm, *My Diary in Mexico,* pp. 5–11. A comprehensive military history of the period is not available in English. Helpful works include Jack A. Dabbs, *The French Army in Mexico, 1861–1867,* and René Chartrand, text, *The Mexican Adventure, 1861–1867,* Osprey Men-At-Arms Series.

16. Sara Yorke Stevenson, *Maximilian in Mexico: A Woman's Reminiscences of the French Intervention, 1862–1867,* pp. 231, 259. Mrs. Stevenson was a fascinating woman in her own right. She became a noted historian, archaeologist, and educator. Her book provides one of the finest impressions of the period available.

17. In the Mexican armies the rank of division general (or general of division) roughly translated to the rank of major general in the U.S. armies. A Mexican brigade general (or general of brigade) roughly translated to a U.S. brigadier. There were also honorific generalships not unlike brevet ranks in the United States.

18. Felix Salm-Salm, *My Diary in Mexico,* pp. 14–15.

19. Ibid., p. 18.

20. Marshal Bazaine returned to Napoleon's good graces in time to lead French forces in the Franco-Prussian War (1870–71). At Metz, he surrendered his entire army of 170,000 men and 1,500 guns. For this he was court-martialed and sentenced to death (later reduced to twenty years' imprisonment). He escaped to Spain, where he died in 1888.

21. Agnes Salm-Salm, *Ten Years of My Life,* pp. 242–43.

22. Ibid., 255; Felix Salm-Salm, *My Diary in Mexico,* pp. 20–22.

23. Agnes Salm-Salm, *Ten Years of My Life,* pp. 255–56.

Chapter 5

1. Felix Salm-Salm, *My Diary in Mexico,* pp. 23–24. Salm's account of the events surrounding Maximilian's march to Querétaro and the subsequent siege is considered one of the most authoritative available.

2. Ibid., pp. 24–31; Samuel Basch, *Memories of Mexico: A History of the Last Ten Months of the Empire,* trans. Hugh McAden Oechler, p. 100. Basch, Maximilian's personal physician, offers another excellent eyewitness account.

3. Felix Salm-Salm, *My Diary in Mexico,* pp. 47–53.

4. Ibid., pp. 56–70; Basch, *Memories of Mexico,* p. 131.

5. Felix Salm-Salm, *My Diary in Mexico,* pp. 72–77.

6. Ibid., pp. 77–79, 88–90. Pitner left a collection of letters and a partial diary

from his Mexican experience contained in Ernst Pitner, *Maximilian's Lieu-tenant: A Personal History of the Mexican Campaign, 1864–1867,* trans. and ed. Gordon Etherington-Smith, with a note on the Mexican background by Don M. Coerver. Unfortunately, a gap in Pitner's writings left no ob-servations from March and April, 1867.

7. Basch, *Memories of Mexico,* pp. 132–38.

8. Felix Salm-Salm, *My Diary in Mexico,* pp. 92–100; *New York Herald,* June 18, 1867.

9. Felix Salm-Salm, *My Diary in Mexico,* pp. 110–33.

10. Agnes Salm-Salm, *Ten Years of My Life,* pp. 257–62.

11. Ibid., pp. 263–80; Porfirio Díaz, *Archivo del General Porfirio Díaz: memorias y documentos,* ed. Alberto Maria Carreño, vol. 3, 46–49.

12. Felix Salm-Salm, *My Diary in Mexico,* pp. 134–45.

13. bid., pp. 147–69.

14. Agnes Salm-Salm, *Ten Years of My Life,* pp. 281–84.

15. Ibid., pp. 284–86. Most Juárez biographers give Agnes scant attention if any, and in regard to her dealings with the president they refer to her ver-sion of events. There are several good studies of Juárez, including Charles Allen Smart, *Viva Juárez! A Biography,* and, more recently, Brian Hamnett, *Juárez.*

16. Felix Salm-Salm, *My Diary in Mexico,* pp. 178–85.

17. *New York Herald,* July 1, 1867.

18. Ibid., pp. 187–218; Basch, *Memories of Mexico,* pp. 175–84; José Luis Blasio, *Maximilian, Emperor of Mexico: Memoirs of His Private Secretary,* trans. and ed. Robert Hammond Murray, with a foreword by Carleton Beals, pp. 155–66. Salm, Basch, and Blasio all provide personal accounts of the final events of the siege, and generally support each other.

19. Agnes Salm-Salm, *Ten Years of My Life,* 286–99; Daniel Moreno, ed., *El Sitio de Querétaro: segun protagonistas y testigos (Sóstenes Rocha, Alberto Hans, Samuel Basch, Princesa Salm-Salm, Mariano Escobedo),* pp. 179–81.

20. Agnes Salm-Salm, *Ten Years of My Life,* pp. 290–92; Felix Salm-Salm, *My Diary in Mexico,* pp. 219–23; Basch, *Memories of Mexico,* pp. 191–92; Blasio, *Maximilian,* pp. 171–72.

21. *New York Herald,* June 11, 1867. This is the only reference found that claimed Agnes to be a relative of President Johnson. Unlike other errone-ous details, this one did not survive as part of her legend.

22. Basch, *Memories of Mexico,* pp. 193–94. Andrew Wheatcroft, *The Habsburgs: Embodying Empire,* p. 180.

23. Felix Salm-Salm, *My Diary in Mexico,* pp. 228–29.

24. Agnes Salm-Salm, *Ten Years of My Life,* pp. 293–96.

25. Felix Salm-Salm, *My Diary in Mexico,* pp. 230–31.

26. Ibid., pp. 231–39.

27. Agnes Salm-Salm, *Ten Years of My Life,* pp. 296–300.

28. Ibid., pp. 301–302; Basch, *Memories of Mexico,* p. 200. Mariano Riva Palacio was the father of popular Republican General Vicente Riva Palacio and not related to Colonel Miguel Palacios.
29. Felix Salm-Salm, *My Diary in Mexico,* p. 236.
30. Ibid., pp. 253–56.
31. Ibid., pp. 259–63.
32. Agnes Salm-Salm, *Ten Years of My Life,* pp. 318–23; Basch, *Memories of Mexico,* pp. 211–12.
33. Ibid.; Agnes Salm-Salm, *Ten Years of My Life,* pp. 321–26.
34. Corti, *Maximilian and Charlotte,* vol. 2, p. 812; Harding, *Phantom Crown,* pp. 316–17; Stevenson, *Maximilian in Mexico,* p. 294; Richard O'Connor, *The Cactus Throne: The Tragedy of Maximilian and Carlotta,* p. 324. The story seems to have been advanced by Count Corti, who gives the source as an Austrian officer (who was not at Querétaro), whose own account, taken from the Vienna National Archives, was admittedly based on hearsay. But Corti writes that Agnes's own account "would lead us to assume that the truth of the above account is almost sure." There is nothing in her account to substantiate such a scene. Of the others, Harding's is simply careless (she refers to the officer as General Vicente Riva Palacio), but is nonetheless colorful: "Agnes Salm shook her golden mane and began to undress. . . . Her white nudity lent a bizarre note to this night that was not made for love." O'Connor takes the most artistic liberty: "she offered herself—her supple equestrienne's body. . . . One glimpse of her splendidly curved torso, under the dim lamp-light . . . was enough for the colonel." Neither Harding nor O'Connor provide sources for their passages.
35. Agnes Salm-Salm, *Ten Years of My Life,* vol. 2, pp. 3–7; Basch, *Memories of Mexico,* p. 212; *New York Herald,* July 11, 1867.
36. Agnes Salm-Salm, *Ten Years of My Life,* vol. 2, pp. 7–9; Felix Salm-Salm, *My Diary in Mexico,* p. 289.
37. Ibid., pp. 283–91.

Chapter 6

1. Stevenson, *Maximilian in Mexico,* pp. 231.
2. Agnes Salm-Salm, *Ten Years of My Life,* vol. 2, pp. 11–12.
3. Smart, *Viva Juárez,* p. 380.
4. Ibid.; Agnes Salm-Salm, *Ten Years of My Life,* vol. 2, pp. 14–16; Smart, *Viva Juárez!,* p. 380; Nereo Rodriguez Barragan, *Juárez and Princess Salm Salm,* trans. M. B. de Barcena, pp. 1–3. Smart writes, "This famous story has been embodied in a painting in San Luis Potosí, but remains wide open to doubt." The painting to which he refers is a 1873 work by Manuel Ocaranza, which depicts Agnes kneeling before Juárez. The event was also

memorialized with life-size wax figures, depicting Agnes and Juárez, in the
Government House in San Luis Potosí, in the same room in which it was
alleged to have occurred.

5. Felix Salm-Salm, *My Diary in Mexico,* vol. 2, 91–103.

6. Ibid., vol. 2, 99–106; Agnes Salm-Salm, *Ten Years of My Life,* vol. 2, pp. 10,
   16–19; Pitner, *Maximilian's Lieutenant,* pp. 187–92. Pitner, Salm, and Major
   Ernst Malburg were among several foreign officers still under guard at
   Querétaro. According to the Austrian Pitner, his companions did not accept their confinement very well: "My two room-mates . . . are Prussians
   and, moreover, endowed with all their bad national qualities. As a result,
   the life of the three of us together is not very pleasant and our conversation is somewhat laconic."

7. Felix Salm-Salm, *My Diary in Mexico,* vol. 2, pp. 107–11.

8. Ibid., pp. 112–60.

9. Ibid., pp. 161–66. The classic biography of Díaz is Carleton Beals, *Porfirio
   Díaz: Dictator of Mexico.* See also Coerver, *The Porfirian Interregnum,* and
   Perry, *Juárez and Díaz.* Díaz indeed seized the presidency by force of arms
   in 1876, although he may well have been elected anyway, and controlled
   Mexico until the revolution of 1910 drove him into exile in Paris. He
   proved quite friendly to United States and European interests.

10. Felix Salm-Salm, *My Diary in Mexico,* vol. 2, pp. 167–68; Agnes Salm-
    Salm, *Ten Years of My Life,* vol. 2, pp. 23–24. Blasio's *Maximilian* contains
    an interesting appendix (pp. 204–209) on the disposition of Maximilian's
    body—it was not well served. Agnes referred frequently to her close rela-
    tionship with Johnson and Seward, but I have found nothing to substanti-
    ate this.

11. Felix Salm-Salm, *My Diary in Mexico,* vol. 2, pp. 168–78.

12. Agnes Salm-Salm, *Ten Years of My Life,* vol. 2, 25–32.

13. Information on the Salm-Salms activities in Europe from 1868–1872 comes
    from Agnes Salm-Salm, *Ten Years of My Life,* vol. 2, pp. 29–280, except
    where noted.

14. For the Franco-Prussian War see Michael Howard, *The Franco-Prussian
    War: The German Invasion of France, 1870–1871.*

15. *American National Biography,* 1999, s.v. "Salm-Salm, Agnes Elisabeth
    Winona Leclercq Joy"; *Times* (London), Sept. 20, 1976. Of her marriage to
    Heneage very little is known, but she never relinquished the name Salm-
    Salm. The Georgette Chamberlain Collection, Duke University, Rare
    Book, Manuscript, and Special Collections Library, contains a travel jour-
    nal from Ms. Chamberlain's visit to Europe in 1897, during which she
    spent the summer with Agnes in Germany. See also Byers, *Twenty Years in
    Europe.*

Epilogue

1. *Vineland (New Jersey) Evening Journal,* Apr. 24, 1899; *Chicago Tribune,* Apr. 23, 1899.

2. Agnes Salm-Salm to William McKinley, Apr. 21, 1899, William McKinley Papers, Library of Congress, Washington, D.C.; George B. Cortelyou to Agnes Salm-Salm, Apr. 21, 1899, William McKinley Papers, Library of Congress, Washington, D.C.

3. *New York Times,* May 15, 1899.

4. *Vineland (New Jersey) Evening Journal,* June 5, 1899, June 24, 1899; *Dictionary of American Biography,* 1935, s.v. "Salm-Salm, Agnes Elisabeth Winona Leclercq Joy;" Agnes Salm-Salm to J. R. Joy, October 15, 1900, Miscellaneous Manuscript Collection, Yale University, Beinecke Rare Book and Manuscript Library. This includes a copy of the dinner program.

5. Clara Barton Collection, Library of Congress, Washington, D.C. This voluminous collection includes many letters between Agnes and Clara Barton, from 1900–1903. They may have met during the Franco-Prussian War or during Agnes's reported trip to America in 1900. They appear to have developed a warm friendship.

6. *Times* (London), Dec. 24, 1912; *New York Times,* Dec. 22, 1912; *American National Biography,* 1999, s.v. "Salm-Salm, Agnes Elisabeth Winona Leclercq Joy."

BIBLIOGRAPHY

Manuscript Collections

Daughters of the American Revolution National Headquarters, Washington, D.C. Agnes Salm-Salm, Application for Membership.

Duke University, Rare Book, Manuscript, and Special Collections Library, Durham, North Carolina. Georgette Chamberlain Collection.

Illinois State Archives, Springfield, Illinois. Commission Register. Richard Yates Correspondence.

Illinois State Historical Society, Manuscript Collection, Springfield, Illinois. Richard Yates Papers.

Library of Congress, Washington, D.C. Clara Barton Collection. James G. Bennett Papers. Frederick Otto von Fritsch Papers. Abraham Lincoln Papers. William McKinley Papers. Theodore Roosevelt Papers. Daniel Sickles Papers. Julius Stahel Papers.

National Archives, Washington, D.C. Edmund Johnson File. Felix Salm-Salm File.

New York State Archives, Albany, New York. Edwin D. Morgan Papers. Ira Harris Papers.

New York State Library, Albany, New York. Edwin D. Morgan Papers.

Rutgers, State University of New Jersey, Archibald Stevens Alexander Library Special Collections and University Archives, New Brunswick, New Jersey. Robert McAllister Papers.

Yale University, Beinecke Rare Book and Manuscript Library, New Haven, Connecticut. Miscellaneous Manuscript Collection.

Books, Articles, and Theses

Adams, Charles Francis. *Charles Francis Adams, 1835–1915: An Autobiography.* New York: Russell & Russell, 1916.

American National Biography, 1999.

Anderson, William Marshall. *An American in Maximilian's Mexico, 1865–1866: Diaries of William Marshall Anderson.* Edited by Ramón Eduardo Ruiz. San Marino, Calif.: Huntington Library, 1959.

Andrews, J. Cutler. *The North Reports the Civil War.* Pittsburgh: University of Pittsburgh Press, 1955.

Appletons' Cyclopedia of American Biography, 1888.

Arms, Florence. *Bright Morning.* Boston: Bruce Humphries, 1962.

Athearn, Robert G. *Thomas Francis Meagher: An Irish Revolutionary in America.* Boulder: University of Colorado Press, 1949.

Barragan, Nereo Rodriguez. *Juárez and Princess Salm Salm.* Translated by M. B. de Barcena. San Luis Potosí: n.p., 1959.

Basch, Samuel. *Memories of Mexico: A History of the Last Ten Months of the Empire.* Translated by Hugh McAden Oechler. San Antonio: Trinity University Press, 1973.

Beals, Carleton. *Porfirio Díaz: Dictator of Mexico.* Philadelphia: J. B. Lippincott Company, 1932.

Blasio, José Luis. *Maximilian, Emperor of Mexico: Memoirs of His Private Secretary.* Translated and edited by Robert Hammond Murray, with a foreword by Carleton Beals. New Haven, Conn.: Yale University Press, 1934.

Boatner, Mark M., III. *The Civil War Dictionary.* Revised ed. New York: Vintage Books, 1988.

Brooks, Noah. *Washington in Lincoln's Time.* New York: The Century Company, 1895.

Burrows, Edwin G., and Mike Wallace. *Gotham: A History of New York City to 1898.* New York: Oxford University Press, 1999.

Burton, William L. *Melting Pot Soldiers: The Union's Ethnic Regiments.* Ames: Iowa State University Press, 1988.

Butterfield, Julia Lorrilard. *A Biographical Memorial of General Daniel Butterfield, Including Many Addresses and Military Writings.* New York: The Grafton Press, 1904.

Byers, S. H. M. *Twenty Years in Europe.* Chicago: Rand McNally & Company, 1900.

Byrne, Frank L., and Andrew T. Weaver, eds. *Haskell of Gettysburg: His Life and Civil War Papers.* Madison: State Historical Society of Wisconsin, 1970.

Camp, Roderic Ai. *Mexican Political Biographies, 1884–1935.* Austin: University of Texas Press, 1991.

Campbell-Shoaf, Heidi S. "Woman of the World: Biography of Princess Agnes Joy Salm-Salm." M.A. thesis, Kent State University, 1994.

Catton, Bruce. *The Army of the Potomac: A Stillness at Appomattox.* Garden City, N.Y.: Doubleday & Company, 1953.

Cavanagh, Michael. *Memoirs of Gen. Thomas Francis Meagher.* Worcester, Mass.: Messenger Press, 1892.

Chamberlain, Joshua Lawrence. *The Passing of the Armies.* New York: G. P. Putnam's Sons, 1915.

Chartrand, René, and Richard Cook. *The Mexican Adventure, 1861–1867.* Osprey Men-At-Arms Series. London: Reed International Books, 1994.

Clinton, Catherine. *The Other Civil War: American Women in the Nineteenth Century.* New York: Hill & Wang, 1984.

Coerver, Don M. *The Porfirian Interregnum: The Presidency of Manuel González of Mexico.* Fort Worth: Texas Christian University Press, 1979.

Coffey, David. "Civil War Royalty: Prince Felix and Princess Agnes Salm-Salm," in *The Human Tradition in the United States,* ed. Steven E. Woodworth. Wilmington, Del.: Scholarly Resources, forthcoming.

———. *John Bell Hood and the Struggle for Atlanta.* Abilene, Tex.: McWhiney Foundation Press, 1998.

Cohen, Richard, "The Lady Vanishes," *Washington Post Magazine,* March 16, 1997, p. 10.

Copps, Frank J., and Thomas J. Curran, eds. *The Immigrant Experience in America.* Boston: Twayne, 1976.

Corti, Count Egon. *Maximilian and Charlotte of Mexico.* 2 vols. New York: Alfred A. Knopf, 1928.

Cunz, Dieter, ed. "Civil War Letters of a German Immigrant." *American-German Review* 11 (October, 1944): 30–33.

Dabbs, Jack A. *The French Army in Mexico, 1861–1867.* The Hague: Mouton, 1963.

Dannett, Sylvia G. L., ed. *Noble Women of the North.* New York: Thomas Yoseloff, 1959.

de Trobriand, Regis. *Four Years with the Army of the Potomac.* Boston: Ticknor & Company, 1889.

Díaz, Porfirio. *Archivo del General Porfirio Díaz: memorias y documentos.* Edited by Alberto Maria Carreño. 29 vols. Mexico, D.F.: Editorial "Elede," 1947–60.

Dictionary of American Biography, 1935.

Donald, David Herbert. *Lincoln.* New York: Simon & Schuster, 1995.

Dyer, Frederick H., comp. *A Compendium of the War of the Rebellion.* Des Moines: Dyer Publishing Co., 1908.

Faust, Drew Gilpen. *Mothers of Invention: Women of the Slaveholding South in the American Civil War.* Chapel Hill: University of North Carolina Press, 1996.

Foote, Shelby. *The Civil War, A Narrative: Fort Sumter to Perryville.* New York: Random House, 1958.

———. *The Civil War, A Narrative: Fredericksburg to Meridian.* New York: Random House, 1963.

———. *The Civil War, A Narrative: Red River to Appomattox.* New York: Random House, 1974.

Ford, Franklin L. *Europe, 1780–1830.* 2d ed. New York: Longman, 1989.

Fritsch, Frederick Otto von. *A Gallant Captain of the Civil War.* Edited by Joseph Tyler Butts. New York: F. Tennyson Neely, 1902.

Fry, James Barnet. *Military Miscellanies.* New York: Brentano's, 1889.

Gil, Carlos B. *The Age of Porfirio Díaz.* Albuquerque: University of New Mexico Press, 1972

Glatthaar, Joseph T. *The March to the Sea and Beyond: Sherman's Troops in the Savannah and Carolina Campaigns.* New York: New York University Press, 1985.

Goldwert, Marvin. "Matías Romero and Congressional Opposition to Seward's Policy toward the French Intervention in Mexico." *The Americas* 22 (1965): 22–40.

Gonzalez, Hector. *Tres libros acerca del Emperador Maximiliano.* Nuevo Leon, Mexico: Centro Literario de Monterrey, 1947.

Gostkowski, Baron. *De Paris a Mexico par les Etats-Unis.* Paris: Tresse & Stock, 1899.

Grant, Ulysses S. *Personal Memoirs.* 2 vols. New York: Charles L. Webster, 1885.

Hamnett, Brian. *Juárez.* London: The Longman Group, 1994.

Hanna, Alfred Jackson, and Kathryn Abbey Hanna. *Napoleon III and Mexico: American Triumph over Monarchy.* Chapel Hill: University of North Carolina Press, 1971.

Harding, Bertita. *Phantom Crown: The Story of Maximilian and Carlota of Mexico.* New York: Halcyon House, 1934.

Harper's Weekly Magazine, May 9, 1863.

Haslip, Joan. *The Crown of Mexico: Maximilian and His Empress Carlota.* New York: Holt, Rinehart and Winston, 1971.

Horn, Stanley F. *The Decisive Battle of Nashville.* Baton Rouge: Louisiana State University Press, 1956.

Horowitz, Murry M. "Ethnicity and Command: The Civil War Experience." *Military Affairs* 42 (December, 1978): 182–89.

Howard, Michael. *The Franco-Prussian War: The German Invasion of France, 1870–1871.* London: Rupert Hart-Davis, 1961.

Hyde, H. Montgomery. *Mexican Empire: The History of Maximilian and Carlota of Mexico.* London: Macmillan & Co. Ltd., 1946.

Johnson, Robert U., and Clarence C. Buel, eds. *Battles and Leaders of the Civil War.* 4 vols. New York: The Century Company, 1884–87.

Joy, James R. *Thomas Joy and His Descendants.* New York: Privately printed, 1900.

Kirk, Charles N., ed. *History of the Fifteenth Pennsylvania Volunteer Cavalry, Which Was Recruited and Known as the Anderson Cavalry in the Rebellion of 1861–1865.* Philadelphia: 1906.

Kollonitz, Countess Paula. *The Court of Mexico.* Translated by J. E. Ollivant. London, 1868.

Krauze, Enrique. *Mexico, Biography of Power: A History of Modern Mexico, 1810–1996.* Translated by Hank Heifetz. New York: HarperCollins, 1997.

Krenkell, John H. ed. *Richard Yates: Civil War Governor.* Danville, Ill.: Interstate Printers & Publishers, 1966.

La Grande Encylopédie, 1985.

Leech, Margaret. *Reveille in Washington, 1860–1865.* New York: Harper & Brothers, 1941.

Leonard, Elizabeth D. *Yankee Women: Gender Battles in the Civil War.* New York: W. W. Norton, 1994.

———. *All the Daring of the Soldier: Women of the Civil War Armies.* New York: W. W. Norton, 1999.

Livermore, Mary A. *My Story of the War: A Woman's Narrative of Four Years Personal Experience As Nurse in the Union Army, and in Relief Work at Home in Hospitals, Camps, and at the Front, During the War of the Rebellion.* Hartford, Conn.: A. D. Worthington, 1889.

Long, E. B., with Barbara Long. *The Civil War Day by Day: An Almanac, 1861–1865.* New York: Doubleday & Co., 1971.

Lonn, Ella. *Foreigners in the Union Army and Navy.* Baton Rouge: Louisiana State University Press, 1951.

Marszalek, John F. *Sherman: A Soldier's Passion for Order.* New York: The Free Press, 1993.

Martin, Percy F. *Maximilian in Mexico: The Story of the French Intervention (1861–1867).* London: Constable & Company, Ltd., 1914.

Massey, Mary Elizabeth. *Bonnet Brigades.* New York: Alfred A. Knopf, 1966; reprinted as *Women in the Civil War.* Lincoln: University of Nebraska Press, 1994.

May, Ernest R. *The Making of the Monroe Doctrine.* Cambridge, Mass.: Harvard University Press, 1975.

McClellan, George B. *McClellan's Own Story.* New York: Charles L. Webster & Company, 1887.

McPherson, James M. *Battle Cry of Freedom: The Civil War Era.* New York: Oxford University Press, 1988.

Meyer, Michael C., and William L. Sherman. *The Course of Mexican History.* 5th ed. New York: Oxford University Press, 1995.

Miller, David L. "Porfirio Díaz and the Army of the East." Ph.D. diss., University of Michigan, 1960.

Moreno, Daniel., ed. *El Sitio de Querétaro: segun protagonistas y testigos (Sóstenes Rocha, Alberto Hans, Samuel Basch, Princesa Salm-Salm, Mariano Escobedo).* Mexico, D.F.: Editorial Porrua, 1982.

Morris, Roy, Jr. *Sheridan: The Life and Wars of General Phil Sheridan.* New York: Crown Publishers, 1992.

Mulholland, St. Clair A. *The Story of the 116th Regiment Pennsylvania Volunteers in the War of the Rebellion.* Edited by Lawrence Frederick Kohl. New York: Fordham University Press, 1996.

National Cyclopedia of American Biography, 1909.

Nelson, Walter Henry. *The Soldier Kings: The House of Hohenzollern.* New York: G. P. Putnam's Sons, 1970.

Niles, Blair. *Passengers to Mexico: The Last Invasion of the Americans.* New York: Farrar and Rinehart, Inc., 1943.

O'Connor, Richard. *The Cactus Throne: The Tragedy of Maximilian and Carlotta.* New York: G. P. Putnam's Sons, 1971.

Perkins, Dexter. *A History of the Monroe Doctrine.* Boston: Little, Brown and Company, 1955.

Perry, Laurens Ballard. *Juárez and Díaz: Machine Politics in Mexico.* DeKalb: Northern Illinois University Press, 1978.

Peterson, Robert L., and John A. Hudson. "Foreign Recruitment for Union Forces." *Civil War History* 7 (June, 1961): 176–89.

Phisterer, Frederick. *New York in the War of the Rebellion, 1861–1865.* 3d ed. 6 vols. Albany, N.Y.: D. B. Lyon Company, State Printers, 1912.

Pitner, Ernst. *Maximilian's Lieutenant: The Personal History of the Mexican*

Campaign, 1864–1867. Translated and edited by Gordon Etherington-Smith, with a note on the Mexican background by Don M. Coerver. Albuquerque: University of New Mexico Press, 1993.

Poole, Annie Sampson. *Mexicans at Home in the Interior.* London: Chapman & Hall, Ltd., 1884.

Porch, Douglas. *The French Foreign Legion: A Complete History of the Legendary Fighting Force.* New York: HarperCollins, 1991.

Quirarte, Martín. *Historiografía Sobre El Imperio de Maximiliano.* Mexico, D.F.: Universidad Nacional Autónoma de México Instituto de Investigaciones Históricas, 1970.

Rice, Owen. "Afield With The Eleventh Army Corps at Chancellorsville." In *Sketches of War History, 1861–1865: Papers Read Before the Ohio Commandery of the Military Order of the Loyal Legion of the United States, 1883–1886.* Cincinnati: Robert Clark & Co., 1888.

Ridley, Jasper. *Maximilian and Juárez.* New York: Ticknor & Fields, 1992.

Robertson, James I., Jr., ed. *The Civil War Letters of General Robert McAllister.* New Brunswick, N.J.: Rutgers University Press, 1965.

Roeder, Ralph. *Juárez and His Mexico.* 2 vols. New York: Viking Press, 1947.

Rolle, Andrew. *The Lost Cause: The Confederate Exodus to Mexico.* Norman: University of Oklahoma Press, 1965.

Ross, Ishbel. *Angel of the Battlefield: The Life of Clara Barton.* New York: Harper & Brothers, 1956.

Salm-Salm, Agnes. *Ten Years of My Life.* 2 vols. London: Richard Bentley & Son, 1876.

Salm-Salm, Felix. *My Diary in Mexico.* 2 vols. London: Richard Bentley, 1868.

Sandburg, Carl. *Abraham Lincoln.* The Sangamon Edition. 6 vols. New York: Charles Scribner's Sons, 1943.

Scott, Joan W. *Gender and the Politics of History.* New York: Columbia University Press, 1988.

———. "Gender: A Useful Category of Historical Analysis." *American Historical Review* 91 (December, 1986): 1053–75.

Sears, Stephen W. *Chancellorsville.* Boston: Houghton Mifflin Company. 1996.

Sheridan, Philip H. *Personal Memoirs of P. H. Sheridan.* 2 vols. New York: Charles L. Webster & Co., 1888.

Sherman, William T. *Memoirs of General William T. Sherman.* 2. vols. New York: Appleton, 1875.

Sifakis, Stewart. *Who Was Who in the Union.* New York: Facts On File, 1988.

Sinkin, Richard N. *The Mexican Reform, 1855–1876: A Study in Liberal Nation Building.* Austin: University of Texas Press, 1979.

Smart, Charles Allen. *Viva Juárez! A Biography.* Philadelphia: J. B. Lippincott Company, 1963.

Stevenson, Sara Yorke. *Maximilian in Mexico: A Woman's Reminiscences of the French Intervention, 1862–1867.* New York: The Century Company, 1899.

Stockhausen, Juliana von. *Agnes de Salm-Salm: Princesse du Mouveau Monde.* Paris: Duculot, 1982.

Struve, Gustav. *Das 8. Regiment N.Y. Freiwilliger und Prinz Felix Salm-Salm.* Washington, D.C.: John F. Riedfeldt, 1862.

Sutherland, Daniel E. *Fredericksburg and Chancellorsville: The Dare Mark Campaign.* Lincoln: University of Nebraska Press, 1998.

Swanberg, W. A. *Sickles the Incredible.* New York: Charles Scribner's Sons, 1956.

Sword, Wiley. *Embrace an Angry Wind: The Confederacy's Last Hurrah, Spring Hill, Franklin, and Nashville.* New York: HarperCollins, 1992.

Tanner, Robert G. *Stonewall in the Valley: Thomas J. "Stonewall" Jackson's Shenandoah Valley Campaign, Spring 1862.* Garden City, N.Y.: Doubleday & Company, 1976.

Tindall, George Brown, and David E. Shi. *America: A Narrative History.* 3d ed. New York: W. W. Norton & Company, 1992.

Tyler, R. Curtis. "Santiago Vidaurri and the Confederacy." *The Americas* 26 (1969): 66–76.

United States War Department. *War of the Rebellion: A Compilation of the Official Records of the Union and Confederate Armies.* 128 vols. Washington, D.C.: Government Printing Office, 1889–1901.

Van Der Heuvel, Gerry. *Mary Todd Lincoln and Varina Howell Davis: The Two First Ladies of the Civil War.* New York: E. P. Dutton, 1988.

Van Deusen, Glyndon G. *William Henry Seward.* New York: Oxford University Press, 1967.

Wainwright, Charles S. *A Diary of Battle: The Personal Journals of Charles S. Wainwright.* Edited by Allan Nevins. New York: Harcourt, Brace and World, 1962.

Warner, Ezra J. *Generals in Blue: Lives of the Union Commanders.* Baton Rouge: Louisiana State University Press, 1964.

Weber, Frank G. "Bismarck's Man in Mexico: Anton von Magnus and the End of Maximilian's Empire." *Hispanic American Historical Review* 46 (1966): 53–65.

Wheatcroft, Andrew. *The Habsburgs: Embodying Empire.* New York: Viking, 1995.

Wiley, Bell Irvin. *The Life of Billy Yank.* Indianapolis: Bobbs-Merrill, 1952.

Wilson, Suzanne Colton, comp. *Column South: With The Fifteenth Pennsylvania Cavalry from Antietam to the Capture of Jefferson Davis.* Edited by J. Ferrell Colton and Antoinette G. Smith. Flagstaff, Ariz.: J. F. Colton & Co., 1960.

Zucker, A. E., ed. *The Forty-Eighters: Political Refugees of the German Revolution of 1848.* New York: Columbia University Press, 1950.

INDEX